TRUMP II

Trump II

Why He Won
What it Means for the World

Tim Hames

First published in Great Britain in 2025 by
Tandem Publishing Ltd

Edited, designed and produced by Tandem Publishing
http://tandempublishing.yolasite.com

ISBN: 978-1-0687613-8-6

10 9 8 7 6 5 4 3 2 1

A CIP catalogue record for this book is available from the British Library.

For Julia, Edward, Tom and George

ACKNOWLEDGEMENTS

This book was in one sense written very swiftly, less than ten full days in November 2024. In another sense, however, it is the product of an intense long-term personal interest in the politics of the United States which started with the contest between the incumbent Jimmy Carter and ex-Governor Ronald Reagan for the presidency in 1980. About a decade later I completed a doctoral thesis on US politics (*Power Without Politics: The Republican National Committee in American Public Life and the debate over party renewal*) and as an academic, a journalist and an independent writer have thought about and have published on American politics ever since. My interests expanded over time to include US foreign policy as well as domestic policy. This includes the US-UK relationship, but of late has focused on US-China too.

I would like to thank a number of people.

The first are my co-founders, colleagues and friends at Acuti Associates, a company that specialises in geopolitics and its ramifications, which we launched in February 2023. Neil Sherlock CBE, Ian Wright CBE and Eileen McGowan (outrageously currently not a CBE) were strong supporters of this volume and commented on the first draft.

The second are another set of friends. Ian Armitage, Tim Farazmand, David Menton, Michael Burke, Diane Rochford and Christine and Robert Ironmonger all merit a (hopefully) honourable mention here.

The third are all those involved with Tandem Publishing who delivered a publication at the speed of a UK general election campaign, not a US one.

Finally, I would like to salute my family, namely my wife Julia (who has become accustomed to crackpot projects such as this), Edward Hardman, Thomas Hardman (who provided technical assistance and also read the initial version of the manuscript) and to George Hames.

It is to these four individuals (and in a way to the American people) that this book is dedicated.

Tim Hames,
January 2025

CONTENTS

INTRODUCTION

A NEW PRODUCTION

*The second Trump term will be much more
than a sequel to his first one*

The political recovery, revival and restoration of Donald Trump as the 47th President of the United States as well as the 45th is an amazing turn of events and an astonishing achievement. It looked extremely improbable on the day that he (somewhat involuntarily) left the Oval Office in 2021. His refusal to concede defeat and approach towards the storming of the Capitol on 6 January 2021 had left his reputation in tatters. Yet he has overcome all this and more to enter the White House again.

The nature of his tenure will not be just a continuation of what occurred when he was last in power. It will be quite different and dramatically so in many respects. The impact of Trump II, furthermore, as will be set out here, will be felt much more strongly in terms of the international economy and across US foreign policy than domestic matters. The scale of this has not been appreciated as it should be.

The fundamental point here is that it would be more appropriate to think of 2025–2029 as a second first term for Mr Trump, not as a conventional second term after an interlude, and this matters a lot.

There are compelling reasons why what is coming might be considered to be a second first term in power.

In his first, first term there were constraints on the president both personally and politically. These would be weaker, indeed might not exist at all, now that he has come back to Washington, D.C.

He had not expected to win the 2016 election (and perhaps did not even want to) and very little preparation had been made for assuming power. This meant the Republican establishment could exercise a substantial influence over major appointments at the Cabinet level, have a degree of sway within the executive office itself and seek to oblige the President to abide by the commitments and obligations of his predecessors. Even members of the First Family (his daughter and his son-in-law) assisted in these efforts. While certain prominent outsiders were appointed, they often did not last long. Mr Trump was only partially his own President. It was on-the-job training on an epic scale.

This will emphatically not be the case in Trump II. Appointments will be based on loyalty to the President personally, not party standing or necessarily obvious qualifications for a position. The chances of recreating the constraints of old look very slim. This will be a show all of its own.

Mr Trump's political programme in 2016 consisted largely of slogans with little in the way of a well-developed project. This again made it possible for him to be steered on policy issues. Over the past four years a cottage industry of pro-Trump think tanks and organisations has emerged, particularly on matters relating to international trade and tariffs. These are his people committed to his philosophy. Trump now has a Trumpism too.

The phrase 'cottage industry' may itself be an understatement. Three institutions are worthy of note. The first is the America First Policy Institute founded shortly after Mr Trump left office. The moving spirits were Larry Kudlow and Linda McMahon, who had served in the Trump Administration, and Brooke Rollins, the Chair and CEO of the organisation. It rapidly expanded its staff to more than 150 people (which is probably more than the employees at all the explicitly political think tanks in the UK combined). It would craft a blueprint for a new Trump term. Ms McMahon would be nominated for Education Secretary and Ms Rollins for Agriculture Secretary. The Heritage Foundation was far older (established in 1973) and had been somewhat aloof from Mr Trump in 2015–2016, with many there doubting his conservative credentials. By 2022, it had converted completely. It produced a 900-page *Project 2025* document which had a particular bent for moving career federal employees over to the status of political appointees of the President of the day. It also, though, made proposals in sensitive areas such as cuts to Medicaid and Medicare (the very popular healthcare programmes aimed at the poor and older citizens respectively) which led Mr Trump to disown it temporarily. It returned to approved status after the November election.

A final, somewhat smaller, institution of note was the Center for Renewing America, again created in 2021, led by Russ Vought who had been the last Director of the Office of Management and Budget in the initial Trump Administration (and who would be nominated to return to that role in the successor one). This is more socially conservative and unapologetically Christian in its mission statement (its credo is 'God, country and community') and it assisted Mr Trump in shoring up his base among the believers.

As a first-term President who aspired to continue in office, Mr Trump had to take account of the effect of his actions, or proposed actions, on his public standing and re-election chances. As he comes back in 2025 this will be far less of a consideration or a constraint. To that extent he is more of a conventional second-term figure, not simply one enjoying a second first term. Yet he is likely to remain atypical. Mainstream second-term Presidents tend to tack to the political centre, and focus on foreign policy with an eye to establishing a reputation as a peacemaker and having a shot at a Nobel Peace Prize; they crave a form of father figure status. Not so for Mr Trump one suspects. His primary concern will be that 'his people' approve of what he does, even if 'his people' are a numerical minority on the issue or question at stake. He will yet again be different.

Despite the above, the impact of a second first Trump term on domestic US politics could be limited. He is likely to find his command over Congress is in a way less potent than it was when first elected.

In 2017–2019, the Republicans enjoyed a comfortable majority of 241–194 in the House of Representatives. Despite recapturing the House in November 2022, their advantage as of Election Day 2024 was a slender 220–215. The combination of their fratricide against their initial choice of Speaker, Kevin McCarthy, and the unedifying search for a replacement, court-ordered redistricting in a number of states and the possibility of a sharp swing against them in two states where they made surprising advances in 2022 (California and New York) meant that it seemed plausible that Mr Trump might win the presidency while the Republicans lost control of the House at the same time. As it would transpire, the strength of the Trump victory at the presidential level was such that Michael Johnson remained House Speaker, and the Republicans retained the same slim majority of 220–215 seats. This meant the new Administration would have far less margin for managerial error in 2025 than it had seen in 2017.

Matters were a little better in the upper chamber. In 2017, the Republicans started with a 52–48 advantage in the Senate, which slipped back to 51–49 after a defeat in a special election in Alabama, before being extended to 53–47 after the 2018 elections. They lost control to a 50–50 divide in 2021 (with Vice President Harris holding the casting vote) and the Democrats managed to nudge that up to a 51–49 lead after the 2022 elections (although two of these 51 were technically independents and two more Senate Democrats would become independents later on). Irrespective of the final presidential outcome, Republicans were well placed to retake the Senate in 2024 with victory all but certain in West Virginia and probable in Montana. Yet, it had long seemed that the ceiling on their performance could be 51–49. Mr Trump might be frustrated by two moderate Republican Senators in Susan Collins (Maine) and Lisa Murkowski (Alaska), much as Joe Biden has been held hostage at times by two renegades of the Democratic caucus in Joe Manchin (West Virginia) and Kyrsten Sinema (Arizona). As it turned out, upset Republican wins in Ohio and Pennsylvania allowed them a 53–47 advantage. This made life easier for a Trump II Administration when it came to confirming key appointments.

Yet, if history is any guide, then the Republicans should anticipate losses (conceivably of scale) in the House of Representatives and even the Senate in the 2026 congressional elections.

All this means that the domestic agenda of a second Trump Administration is destined to focus on:

- Full authorisation of a border wall between the US and Mexico (which he will probably get).
- A sizeable and targeted tax cut aimed at lower income Americans (which should be obtainable).
- An attempt to reconstitute the federal bureaucracy (and 'deep state'). This may be impossible.

- An even more comprehensive drive to shape the federal judiciary through appointments (he would probably have at least one Supreme Court appointment, with Clarence Thomas likely to retire, and may have the chance to choose a successor to Chief Justice John Roberts too).
- A concerted effort at deregulation, reversing many of the measures of the Biden era.
- A repudiation of the Net Zero agenda, such as subsidising development of electric cars.

As will be set out in Chapter Six, this still means that Trump II will have a substantial effect within the United States itself. The larger shockwaves will, nonetheless, be felt elsewhere and across the world.

Almost all second-term US Presidents are more active in foreign affairs as they reach the end of their time as Chief Executive, although normally they seek to achieve success as a perceived peacemaker. A second Trump Administration will also be more active in foreign matters, but quite distinctly.

A restored President Trump would be more ambitious and forceful in this sphere than in his first term.

- Sweeping and systematic tariffs of an across-the-board form can be anticipated, along with other protectionist measures and a hostile disregard towards the World Trade Organization.
- A similar reluctance to engage with, let alone work through, other multilateral economic or quasi-economic entities such as the IMF, the World Bank and the G7 is a racing certainty.
- The direction of fiscal policy under Mr Trump might well convince the US Federal Reserve to proceed

more cautiously in reducing interest rates in 2025. This in turn would have an impact on the interest rate environment internationally and influence key exchange rates.

A second Trump Administration will be an extension of, not just a continuation of, the first one. Among the initiatives and instincts that could be expected are the following:

- A withdrawal of active US military support for Ukraine and acceptance of a settlement in that country which involves territorial concessions to Vladimir Putin and Russia.
- A 'work to rule' approach to NATO until the Europeans pay more for the cost of it.
- A highly antagonistic attitude with regards to China on the political and economic fronts.
- A much more aggressive stance towards Iran with periodic drone strikes to make the point.
- A total disavowal of the Paris Accord and wider international climate change programme.
- A possible resumption of his idiosyncratic engagement with the regime in North Korea.
- A pattern of 'picking favourites' among countries and leaders that seem most aligned with his outlook. This favourable treatment would be extended to Italy, Hungary and Slovakia in Europe (to the intense discomfort of the EU), Argentina in South America and to Israel and Saudi Arabia in the Middle East. Other Trumpian movements would be embraced.

Much of the above will be broadly popular within the US itself (if viewed with alarm in the Senate) and very little of it would require the active assent of Congress or be susceptible to obstruction by it.

The objectives and output of a new Trump Administration can be traced in advance. Despite this, not only many governments but a vast swathe of the international business community (including in the UK) appear to be in denial about the possibilities, disinclined to engage in intelligent planning for how to prepare for highly disruptive activity with regards to international economics and politics or, worse still, have opted for a 'wake me up when those four years are over' approach to the matter.

This is fundamentally mistaken. The purpose of this volume is to set out why Mr Trump pulled off such an apparently improbable election victory and what will happen to the world next as a result.

CHAPTER ONE

THE UNIQUE POLITICAL APPEAL OF DONALD TRUMP

*A businessman turned media celebrity turned
presidential candidate*

Donald Trump has been a major figure in American public life for the better part of five decades and a substantial personality for in excess of 35 years. He was born on 14 June 1946 (and thus a classic 'baby boomer') as the fourth child of Fred Trump, a very successful figure in the property sector, and Mary Anne MacLeod Trump (to whom he seems to have been especially close). He was also the second son, not the anticipated heir. His sibling, Fred Trump Jr, was conscripted into the business against his will (he wanted to be and would become an airline pilot, which his father held in contempt). He split from the family, endured alcoholism and died at the tender age of 42 in 1981.

Donald Trump, even by then the new hope for his father, attended Fordham University and then went to the Wharton School at the University of Pennsylvania where he majored in business and economics. Once he had completed his studies and, like many of his generation who could, avoided involvement in the Vietnam War, he returned to take up a senior position in what was then called Trump Management.

The company that he became part of in 1968 was a very profitable but perhaps slightly dull entity which concentrated on the management and renovation of buildings, residential

1

and commercial. Although he had an older brother, the young Donald was clearly the one with the entrepreneurial touch and by 1971 (at the age of 25) had become the President of what he renamed as The Trump Organization. This was an indicator that he intended to expand the corporate horizons wider, well beyond its historic territory.

He did so, as he famously put it himself, with the assistance of 'a small loan of a million dollars' from his father that he would be compelled to return with interest. He might or might not have done so but certainly obtained substantial additional funding from Fred Trump over the years. He may be a truly brilliant businessman, but it would be a stretch to say he had to bootstrap it.

He first really captured the public imagination in 1978 with an audacious scheme to renovate the Commodore Hotel, a defunct building adjacent to the Grand Central Terminal. Its location means that it was familiar to virtually all who lived and/or worked in New York City. It re-opened as the Grand Hyatt Hotel in 1980 and was visually and commercially very appealing.

In the same year he acquired the right to develop Trump Tower, which was again right in the heart of New York City. To state that no expense was spared on this project would be putting it mildly. It stood out in part because it was an act of defiance against the apparent decline of New York. The city had teetered on the edge of outright financial ruin in the 1970s, with the powers that be in Washington, D.C. disinclined to step in and to save it (triggering the memorable newspaper headline about the attitude of the then President, 'Ford to City: Drop Dead'). Crime was high and the metropolis appeared all but ungovernable. Under Mayor Ed Koch, a popular figure with some swagger, and the improvised 'I Love New York' advertising campaign, it was making a comeback.

Donald Trump added much-needed colour to this (mostly gold). His architecture had, therefore, a wider significance. In 1988 he took on the Plaza Hotel but bit off rather more than he could chew: the expenditure involved, the scale of the loans solicited, and the impact of recession in the early 1990s took him by 1995 to the brink of bankruptcy.

The Trump Organization had hence moved out of the maintaining and renovation of often less than entirely attractive real estate into much more flamboyant terrain. Hotels would, though, be the start of matters. They would continue to be a strategic objective (the Trump International Hotel and Tower in Chicago, opened in 2008, being a case study in point) but the man at the helm was looking to extend his empire into other, but usually related, sectors.

The first of these was casinos. Mr Trump entered, with a not atypical splash, into Atlantic City, New Jersey, supposedly the Las Vegas of the North (although with none of the arid Nevada climate). This was booming territory in the 1980s but on less certain foundations in the 1990s. It was also challenging to operate in territory where rivals had strong links to organised crime. This would not prove to be a long-term core element in his commercial portfolio. He did learn from it.

A different area which was more attractive and had greater staying power was private clubs. In an act of genuine foresight The Trump Organization acquired Mar-a-Lago in Florida in 1985 and ten years later it became the private club and resort that it is now. Whether it makes money on a day-to-day basis is disputable but there is no doubt that the value of the site has soared since its acquisition and that it would sell for an astonishing sum were it ever to come on the market. After he left the White House in January 2021, the then ex-President would soon abandon Trump Tower in New York as his personal base and relocate (and change his voting registration) to his Florida abode. In his coming second term it will certainly serve as the second White House at weekends and other occasions. It will be a case of Goodbye Camp David. Hello Camp Donald.

One feature of the Mar-a-Lago estate is its acclaimed golf course, and that sport was where the Trump attention turned next. He saw the potential in up-scale golf locations, whether they be of a historic nature or a blank sheet that would allow him to create an enticing eighteen holes (the nineteenth would invariably be a revenue spinner too, although Mr Trump himself does not touch alcohol). From 1999, his business started building and buying golf courses in the United States and elsewhere (notably Scotland which brought the then First Minister, the late Alex Salmond, into deliberations and negotiations with Mr Trump, which would have been fascinating to watch, as two arch showmen circled each other). As of late 2024, The Trump Organization owns fourteen golf courses and manages another three. Although the accounts of the Trump business are complicated, opaque and often secretive, it can be assumed that this has been an effective investment for him, a new string to his bow.

His other forays into sport have been less lucrative. His experiments with ownership of an American Football team, involvement with boxing and, somewhat bizarrely, cycling (the person who thought that establishing a Tour de Trump in the United States was a fabulous idea surely needed their head examined). Baseball and basketball have not secured the Trump attention.

His exploration of what might be loosely described as leisure and entertainment went better. From 1996 to 2015 he owned all or part of the Miss Universe pageants, including Miss USA and Miss Team USA. This was initially in collaboration with the CBS network and then NBC, until that station decided that changing social attitudes meant that it wanted to exit this particular field. In political terms it is probably best remembered for salacious suggestions (the subject of a lawsuit in the UK which Mr Trump lost) as to what might have occurred in a hotel bathroom in Moscow at the time of Miss Universe in 2013. Until time ran out on beauty contests, nevertheless, this was a net positive for his portfolio.

Some of the other offshoots did not stand the test of time or they fell foul of adverse lawsuits. He briefly controlled an airline, the Trump Shuttle, which in terms of his finances, if not it should be stressed literally, crash-landed. In 2004 he co-founded Trump University, which sold real estate seminars and degree courses at an initial cost of $35,000, but their academic status and value for money were challenged and he was obliged to rebrand as the Trump Entrepreneur Institute in 2010 as part of an out-of-court settlement and he seems to have lost interest in it since. He had a short excursion into philanthropy via the Donald J. Trump Foundation as early as 1988, but his erratic cash-flow among other factors meant that it did not acquire much in the way of scale. If he had not opted to seek the presidency, he would doubtless have found yet more domains in which to establish The Trump Organization as an actor and to remorselessly promote its brand.

Promotion and publicity (or 'free media' in the parlance) have been central to his activities. This started with his willingness to be a staple for the New York newspaper tabloids, who revelled in his every deed and his intriguing private life, be it his marriage to (and ultimate divorce from) his first wife, the photogenic Czech Ivana Zelnickova, the mother of Donald Jr, Ivanka and Eric, and then her successor Marla Marples (or 'the Georgia Peach' as the sub-editors dubbed her), who would last for a shorter period but produced a daughter, Tiffany (an argument of a sort rages as to whether she was named after the store or not). His third marriage to Melania Krauss, which has endured for almost twenty years now, did not devour quite as many column inches but it did lead to a final child, Barron, whose surname and height (6' 7") make him destined for fame.

What really secured attention for him beyond New York was his enthusiasm for writing about himself. There have been no fewer than nineteen books under his name (frequently with a co-author, who it is possible spent most of the time at the keyboard). The first of these volumes, *The Art of the Deal*, published in 1987, was a massive bestseller and in many ways changed the entire character of the business book market. His partner with the pen was Tony Schwartz, and although the style is perhaps a little dated it remains a classic of its form. It had a reach that went well beyond the five boroughs and was read by aspiring business tycoons across the US.

It is an immensely revealing manuscript. The tone is set by a hurricane of an opening chapter. Titled 'Dealing: A Week in the Life', it presents what Mr Trump does over five notional days (actual dates are not specified).

The preamble accurately anticipates his methodology as President three decades or so later. He states:

'Most people are surprised at the way I work. I play it very loose. I don't carry a briefcase. I try not to schedule too many meetings. I leave my door open. You can't be imaginative as an entrepreneur if you've got too much structure. I prefer to come to work each day and see what develops.'

What this means is:

'There is rarely a day with fewer than fifty [telephone] calls, and it often runs to a hundred. In between, I have at least a dozen meetings. The majority of them occur on the spur of the moment, and few of them last longer than fifteen minutes.'

The diary itself shows the scope of his activities and involves what is less name-dropping than name-carpet-bombing of famous Americans with whom he has calls or direct in-person conversations.

On Monday, for example, we learn that he is friendly with Mario Cuomo, then Governor of New York (but not, we will discover later, with Ed Koch, the Mayor of New York City). Don Imus (a radio host), Tom Brokaw (a television newscaster), Gerry Schoenfeld (theatre impresario) and Lee Iacocca (the CEO of Chrysler and a potential candidate for the 1988 Democratic presidential nomination) are all cited.

On Tuesday he has a call with Ivan Boesky, a Wall Street titan, but 'I have no idea that two weeks from now, Boesky will plead guilty to insider trading.' In the afternoon 'Michael Milken, the guy who invented junk-bond trading at Drexel, has called me for several years [and does so again that day], I have no idea that Drexel is about to get enmeshed in the insider-trading scandal that will soon rock Wall Street … I think that Mike's a brilliant guy.'

In the midst of all this there are calls with Dave Winfield (a baseball legend), Larry Csonka (a former American football player), Calvin Klein, Senator John Danforth and Diana Ross finds herself noted.

Come Wednesday, in the morning we are informed that Mar-a-Lago, his Florida retreat, had been built in the early 1920s by Marjorie Merriweather Post, heiress to the Post cereal fortune and at the time Mrs Edward F. Hutton. The estate has 118 rooms and 'Three boatloads of Dorian stone were brought from Italy for the exterior walls and 36,000 Spanish tiles dating back to the fifteenth century were used on the exterior and interior.'

When she died, Mrs Post left it to the federal government as a proposed presidential retreat. That did not happen (although it did in the end) and it went back to her survivors.

They put it on the market for $25 million. Mr Trump bided his time and lets us know in this section that he picked it up for $5 million in cash and $3 million for the furnishings. He plainly appreciates how to drive a hard bargain.

The afternoon offers, considering the events to come much later, this intriguing story:

'A prominent businessman who does a lot of business with the Soviet Union calls to keep me posted on a construction project. The idea got off the ground after I sat next to the Soviet Ambassador, Yuri Dubinin [whose daughter was an admirer of Trump Tower] … One thing led to another, and now I'm talking about building a large luxury hotel, across the street from the Kremlin, in partnership with the Soviet government. They have asked me to go to Moscow in July.'

For a little variety, a call with the author Judith Krantz occurs and Estée Lauder enters the narrative.

Thursday is comparatively quiet. It starts with 'A friend of mine, a highly successful and very well-known painter, comes to say hello and to invite me to an opening.' It becomes obvious this is Jackson Pollock. In the afternoon, Mr Trump is working on plans for the world's tallest building to be erected by him in New York City (alas, it never was). In the evening, though, he and his wife have been invited to dinner by John, Cardinal O'Connor, at St Patrick's Cathedral. It is hard, he writes, 'not to be a little awed'.

By Friday, he is winding down. His most pressing task is his application for a Nevada gaming licence. He is informed that he has to provide some character references. He selects General Pete Dawkins; Benjamin Holloway, Chairman and CEO of Equitable Real Estate Group; and Conrad Stephenson of Chase Manhattan Bank. Oh, he reflects further, 'Also … put down John, Cardinal O'Connor.'

His last engagement involves an apparently impromptu

visit by David Letterman, the TV comic host.

It is not a stretch to discern why *The Art of the Deal* became a top bestseller.

It has led to something of a conveyor belt of words ever since. Among the other books (whose titles usually indicate what exists within the covers) have also been *Trump Surviving At the Top, Trump: The Art of the Comeback, Trump: How to Get Rich, Trump 101: The Way to Success*, and *Think Big and Kick Ass* (no virtue in subtlety in this section of the literary landscape). Since he departed the White House, the output has flowed once more with *Our Journey Together* (2021), *Letters to Trump* (2023) and *Save America* (2024) all rolling off the production line. He had not, significantly, produced a definitive memoir as such, dismissing suggestions that he might do so after 2021 presumably because he believed *Trump: The Art of the Comeback* remained viable. If so, he was correct. He also refused to discuss establishing his Presidential Library on that logic.

There is one other critical piece of the jigsaw as to why Donald Trump entered the campaign trail with a highly unusual prior level of name recognition and appeal to the sympathy of voters. Indeed, without it, his shot at the White House in 2016 might well have fallen short of victory.

It is the time that he spent as the host of *The Apprentice* between 2004–2015. It predated the version that is well known in the United Kingdom by a year and, while both have been a hit with a large slice of the television audience, the formula and styles of the two hosts – Mr Trump and initially Sir Alan, then Lord Alan, Sugar – are somewhat different. Lord Sugar does have a classic rags-to-riches narrative to his life, initially made his money in technology but then buttressed his bank balance through the property sector, and his one jaunt into sports finance (his ownership of Tottenham

Hotspur FC) left him with heartburn. His persona on the show is gruff and grumpy. He allows his assistants sufficient space that they have become stars in their own right. The US take on *The Apprentice* was from the first episode far closer to being *The Donald Trump Show*. It could be crass, but it was compelling watching. It allowed Mr Trump to reach millions more of his fellow citizens than he would have done otherwise. It was his own apprenticeship for power.

What can be deduced from all this about Mr Trump as a commercial figure and a candidate?

The first aspect, obvious but worth elaborating on, is that there is no shortage here of ambition, innovation or a willingness to take risks, sometimes dangerous ones, to advance his agenda along with a certain acceptance that some of these innovations will fall flat on their face.

The objective of The Trump Organization (and the man himself) was to be a conglomerate. The strategy has been consistent and coherent even if the tactics have appeared anarchic and impulsive. While exactly how wealthy he is and whether he would have been richer still if he has just invested the family funds in the stock market and stuck to repairing tired New York buildings is a matter of considerable discussion, it cannot be disputed that he has built a massive company. This has involved taking big chances for high stakes and winning more often than he is losing.

In that light, there are similarities between Mr Trump and what might otherwise strike one as a completely opposite individual, namely Sir Richard Branson. He started in the music industry and has branched out into an airline, inter-city train transportation and financial services and much more. Some of his ideas, Virgin Weddings and Virgin Vodka for example, did not do much for him. What worked well for him comfortably compensated for those mistaken detours. If he had decided to enter British politics, there might have been many willing to lend him their ballots.

The core distinction is that Sir Richard has always cultivated the impression of the bohemian businessman, the hippy entrepreneur. It is largely thought likely that his political views are on the centre-left and the US politician with whom he has a close friendship is Barack Obama. Like Mr Trump, he has an exceptional flair for seducing sections of the media. He has become a type of national treasure, even though his personal and corporate accounts are little less of a mystery than those of the 45th and 47th President. Mr Trump really does not do bohemian. He does brash. His mode would not work in UK elections. Sir Richard's may not catch fire in the United States.

The second factor is that Mr Trump is at the end of the day a team of one. He has associates and aides and an army of lawyers (it has been estimated that he has been involved in over 4,000 lawsuits in his life) and there are close family members who he listens to (his daughter Ivanka was a key figure in his first term of office but has withdrawn from the public realm since then) but there is no guru, let alone a Svengali lurking out there. This will not change in his additional term as President.

The third is that Mr Trump plainly has no problem with debt as a means of financing an ambition. Traditional Republicans rather recoil at debt in either the private or the federal financial theatre. Mr Trump was more than content last time to champion a tax cutting programme that, in the short-term at least, but probably in the longer-term too, involved the United States government steering a very long way from the balanced budget which was once an almost religious ideal. He is not about to become a slave to that orthodoxy during his next outing in Washington, D.C.

The fourth is that he has always been ahead of the curve when it comes to media presentation. When New York City newspapers still sold widely they were the target of his attention (and the source of his introduction to Rupert Murdoch through his bombastic *The New York Post*). He all but reinvented the business book as a personal vehicle via *The Art of the Deal*. He took over television through imposing himself at the centre of the stage in *The Apprentice*. It should have been no surprise from all this that he would be the first presidential contender to make his Twitter feed a primary means of communication with a huge number of American electors. His embrace of his own version of it – Truth Social or TRUTH Social – duly established by the Trump Media and Technology Group after his expulsion from Twitter, fits the pattern of his approach.

Finally, Mr Trump's interest in politics and elections did not come to him suddenly in advance of the 2016 election. It had been incubating for a lengthy period of time. As early as 1987 he took out full-page newspaper advertisements to set out his ideas on foreign policy and (ironically) on how to eliminate the federal budget deficit. In mid-1988 he apparently let Lee Atwater, campaign manager for Vice President George H. W. Bush, know that he would allow his name to be placed on the list of possible running-mates for the November election. Mr Bush, when told, thought the notion was mad (but as he ended up selecting Senator Dan Quayle instead it may have been less ludicrous than at first blush).

Mr Trump was a registered Republican from 1987 to 1999, but fell out of love with them. Between 1999 and 2001 he aligned with the new Reform Party (and for a few months half-heartedly pursued their 2000 presidential nomination). In 2001 all the way through to 2009 (so the entirety of the tenure of President George W. Bush) he was a registered

Democrat. He swapped back to the GOP (the Republicans) in 2009 at almost the instant that the Obama Administration landed in office. In 2011 he openly toyed with running against the new President and loudly stated as much in a speech to the Conservative Political Action Committee (CPAC) annual conference in that year but, when he obtained no support of note, dropped that notion and re-assigned as an Independent. By 2012 he was a Republican once more. That amounts to six switches in political party alignment in a 25-year period. No other US President is thought to have had more than one (Ronald Reagan was a Democrat). His ability once in politics to cut across party lines in the US electorate should be no shock at all. He has been everywhere.

The above story aids an explanation of the unique political appeal of Donald J. Trump. Three further considerations also have an important place in his rise to be a credible contender.

The first is that the idea of the outsider as a political saviour has a very long history in the United States and is notably embedded in the Republican Party more than any other. The first American President, George Washington, was a military commander not a professional politician. After the US Civil War, the Republicans turned to Ulysses Grant as President from 1869–1877. The surge in support for Teddy Roosevelt started with his status as a military adventurer. In the aftermath of World War I, the business acumen of Herbert Hoover was his calling card for high office. In 1940, desperate for a figure who might at least restrain the likely third term triumph of Franklin D. Roosevelt (who was definitely a professional politician), the Republicans turned to Wendell Willkie, a famed corporate executive with no prior elective or political record, to be their leader. In 1952, Dwight D. Eisenhower moved directly from the military into politics.

As will be observed later, General Eisenhower was something of an exception during the Cold War era of presidential elections. Jesse Jackson in 1984 and 1988 and Pat Robertson in 1988 tested the water for preacher-politicians. Since the fall of the Berlin Wall and the implosion of the USSR, outsider candidacies have been all the rage. Ross Perot stood as an independent in 1992 (but mostly obtained his support from disillusioned Republicans) and won almost a fifth of the vote (he would stand again in 1996 but far less effectively). In the Republican primary campaigns of 1996 and 2000 Steve Forbes, a neophyte political figure offering his 'flat tax' as the solution to all national discontent, made the running for a while in both contests. In 2004, this time for the Democrats, there was a boomlet for General Wesley Clark for the presidency.

In 2008 and 2012 Mitt Romney stood as much on his record as a successful business figure and the man who turned around the fortunes of the Salt Lake City Winter Olympic Games as he did on his resume as a one-term Governor of what is staunchly Democratic Massachusetts. Herman Cain, a black entrepreneur with zero political form, blazed a trail for a while in 2012 too. In the 2016 Republican field (and there were 17 names in the frame at one stage), Mr Trump had some competition on the outsider front from Ben Carson, a neurosurgeon with a television following. In 2020, Michael Bloomberg, a businessman turned Mayor of New York, put himself forward for the Democrats (who were not having it). In 2024, one of Mr Trump's opponents (although he did not come across as an enemy) was Vivek Ramaswamy, who made his millions in technology. The prospective field for the GOP in 2028 should be thankful that Elon Musk (who was born in South Africa) is not constitutionally capable of sending his own rocket into an electoral orbit.

There is, to surmise, no originality in being an outsider. The novelty of Mr Trump is him winning.

Second, the themes which Mr Trump articulated, although seemingly in contrast to more recent Republican political thinking, have long roots in that party and its philosophy over time. The core traits of the Republican Party at its creation (set out magisterially in *The Origins of the Republican Party 1852–1856* by William E. Gienapp, originally published in 1987, the same year as *The Art of the Deal*, though the Trump tome sold far more copies) were what could be counted today as nativism and nationalism, isolationism and unilateralism, protectionism and populism (emancipating the slaves back then was a minority consideration).

These continued to be at the heart of the Republican Party outlook in the several decades after the Civil War, when it customarily held the White House with only Grover Cleveland and Woodrow Wilson occupying it for the Democrats between 1865 and 1933. The Republican Administrations of the 1920s continued to believe in robust tariffs, were suspicious of international alliances (which meant that the United States remained outside of the League of Nations, a fatal blow to it), and wanted to contain immigration thought undesirable (that of Irish/Eastern European Roman Catholics). Much of this changed after 1945 but it was never completely eradicated. Whenever the Republicans found themselves in opposition they were tempted to return to it.

Third, the Republican ideology that had replaced the previous prevailing set of principles was to suffer a meltdown during the eight years that George W. Bush was the resident of the White House. His Administration started with the assertion that free markets, open trade and light-touch regulation were the essence of economic vitality and, after the attacks of September 11 2001, and the seeming rout of Al Qaeda in Afghanistan, that a muscular application of hard power in international affairs was the new overarching doctrine in foreign policy, with the so-called 'Vietnam Syndrome' tamed. It also professed to be committed to the cause that most social and religious conservatives held dear: the overturn of the controversial landmark *Roe v Wade* 1973 on abortion, via Supreme Court appointments.

Yet when Mr Bush returned to private life, the political outlook he had stood for was in very poor shape. The global financial crisis and near collapse of the US economy in late 2008 had shattered faith in the approach to the economy that Republicans since Ronald Reagan had been associated with. The debacle and the quicksand that the occupation of Iraq (and to a lesser degree Afghanistan) had become meant that shares in the neo-conservative worldview of US foreign policy had sunk to bargain basement levels. After eight years of his presidency and two appointments to the bench, *Roe v Wade* was still the reality.

All of this meant that the chance was there for someone to come along and conduct what was close to a hostile take-over of a Republican Party that had clearly lost its way. The stirrings of a 'back to basics' revival came with the Tea Party movement after the 2008 election defeat, but it lacked a personality to head it, and it struggled to find a comprehensive proactive prospectus.

Into the void would step one Donald Trump … but he needed one huge other change to assist him.

CHAPTER TWO

THE GREAT FRAGMENTATION

*A fundamentally changed international order
opened the door to Donald Trump*

As the last chapter set out, the personality and the profile of Donald Trump, the history of the themes which he came to articulate within the Republican Party, the equally long-standing party constituency for an 'outsider' as the champion for conservative values, and the collapse of what had been the key components of Republican thinking during the second term of George W. Bush as US President all created a theoretical opportunity for Mr Trump to seize the party nomination in 2016.

For him to move beyond that and actually capture the Oval Office required something much bigger still. The rules of the game would have to be changed in a wholesale fashion. If not, then Mr Trump would have been not much more than a novelty contender in 2016 and scarcely much better than that when he sought his political resurrection in 2024. What was needed, and what has occurred over the past ten years or so, was for the entire international system to be systematically transformed.

The critical word here is 'systematically'. Systems largely shape who are politically credible people. The breakdown of what had been an established system allowed new actors and new agendas once thought to be manifestly outside of the mainstream – even extreme – to be seen in a new light. Mr

Trump has been a very well-known figure in American public life for several decades now. Yet if he had thrown his hat in the ring as a presidential aspirant in, say, 1988 as an alternative to then Vice President Bush as the Republican candidate, or in 2000 against his son, the Governor of Texas, when he launched his own bid to become Commander-in-Chief, or as late as 2008 when the prospect of being the Republican on the presidential ballot was perhaps not so appealing, he would have attracted attention but it is extremely doubtful that he would have won. Outsiders could, and indeed regularly did, come from nowhere to become Senators or Governors or in the House of Representatives but the presidential stage demanded a sense of formal qualification which Mr Trump did not have. Circumstances had to evolve in a manner that made their absence less consequential.

The Cold War era (1945–1990) set the boundaries within which American presidential elections took place. It was an age for professional politicians, largely those who had served an apprenticeship as Vice President (as Harry Truman, Richard Nixon, Lyndon Johnson, Gerald Ford and George H. W. Bush had all done) or as the Governor of a very large state (Ronald Reagan from California). Where the professional politician concerned did not have that background, such as Jimmy Carter, a one-term Governor from Georgia, a state that was somewhat smaller and less significant then than it is now, the experience was not a happy one. At least he prevailed once. Others with slender claims to be US President such as Barry Goldwater, an Arizona Senator, in 1964, or George McGovern, a South Dakota Senator, in 1972, would be utterly crushed when they offered themselves on the national stage. The only 'outsider' to enter the equation in this era, Dwight D. Eisenhower, was, as the former commander of Allied forces at D-Day and then the first military leader of

NATO, not that much of an outsider really, as the demands of the Cold War suited what he had to offer the voters. If somehow the Cold War had been avoided after 1945 the constituency for him might well have been considerably smaller and he either would not have felt it his duty to run or have had less chance. The idea of a businessman as a different sort of acceptable outsider simply was not there (in contrast to the inter-war period when corporate chiefs were definitely on the list of possible GOP contenders).

The international environment for the 25-plus years from 1990 was clearly different. It was defined by a system of authority in which the United States was the sole economic, political, military, technological and cultural superpower, and with this was an overwhelming elite agreement that this was a state of affairs that the United States should welcome and that it was the responsibility of whoever served as President to ensure it continued to be an entrenched authority.

Other states might make partial claims to pre-eminence in one or other of the five domains, but none could come close to being a serious competitor to the US in all of them. In truth, no nation was even devising a determined approach to mount such a challenge. Russia was a basket case after 1990. China was a very long way from acquiring the basic building blocks to take on the United States. India was an intriguing possible global player but not for several decades yet to come. Japan, which at one stage in the 1980s serious people thought might be in a position to take over from the US as the largest and most successful economy on the planet, was instead about to enter a prolonged era of relative economic stagnation, and it would not develop the sorts of companies that would be technologically transformative as the likes of Microsoft, Apple, Amazon, Google or Facebook proved to be. Britain and France had by the 1980s largely arrested what been a depressing decline on multiple fronts over the previous four decades, but were plainly not rivals to the US. Germany had a strong economy but also had a history which was a ball and chain beyond that. The European Union was at best a slow work in progress. It also acknowledged the *Pax Americana*.

The area of the world where this outcome was accepted least, and hence the location of the most tension, was, crucially, the Middle East and notable nearby nations. Even here, the enemies of the United States were either rogue states whose regimes did not have much of an export market to them (Iraq, Iran and Syria) or were rogue organisations such as Al Qaeda which had huge limitations to them. As a result, this American-dominated architecture survived the Gulf War of 1991, the many various Balkan conflicts of the 1990s, the terrorist attacks on the US in 2001, the Iraq War of 2003 and the global financial crisis of 2008–2009. Indeed, the term 'survived' vastly understated matters. The distance between the US and its rivals in economic terms had been expanded. The same was true for politics and diplomacy. The US defence budget was larger than all other players combined. To all intents and purposes America owned the internet revolution. It dominated cultural spheres.

It was one of three pillars on which a benign economic regime was secured. Another was the taming of inflation in the developed world, largely credited to the enhanced autonomy of central banks. The last spike of inflation worthy of note had been at the very beginning of the 1990s when an oil price shock related to the invasion of Kuwait by Iraq induced both price increases and a recession in the manner of (but not with the intensity of) those associated with the 1970s and 1980s. After that, the central banks, whose increased independence was a feature of life across democracies, ruled the roost. Monetary policy was now considered the most important aspect of economic activity while fiscal policy (the area that politicians still had some control over) was seen as a secondary area.

The final aspect was a liberal trading order which had incorporated China's integration into the global economy, an event with an immense effect as it allowed for robust global growth without inflation. While there would be some protestors for protectionism, they huffed and puffed from the side-lines. The intellectual consensus behind free and ever-expanding trade reinforced international economics. The core feature of the centre-left and its leadership, be it the United States under Bill Clinton, Tony Blair in the United Kingdom or Gerhard Schröder in Germany was that it promoted globalisation and all that came along with it (including sizeable economic migration) with the zeal of the converted. It was the hallmark of the so-called 'Third Way'. Free trade appeared to have swept all before it. This was as true in the academic fraternity as it was at the ballot box. There might be a few individuals left who were willing to accept the label of 'protectionist' but they often tried to soften that association with the insistence that all they were advocating was 'fair trade', and in any case they appeared to have the intellectual standing and political authority of the Flat Earth Society.

A force demands a phrase to summarise it. The term that eventually acquired that status was 'The Great Moderation'. These words started life within a relatively technical paper published in the US by two economists, James Stock and Mark Watson, in 2002. They observed that the business cycle in most advanced countries seemed to have become longer, smoother and less extreme in its content. They then tested a set of potential explanations for this outcome, exclusively economic, not political.

As a concept, The Great Moderation would enter a period of hibernation. It was revived when Ben Bernanke, then a member, but soon to become the Chairman, of the Federal Reserve Board, took it as a theme for a speech he delivered in 2004. The Great Moderation had found a constituency.

It was from here that others started to stitch together the political and economic features of it. The post-Cold War international structure was the platform that made economic stability viable. The comparative success of the economic policies then embraced had allowed free trade to flourish. It appeared at one stage that the global financial crisis of 2008 might bring The Great Moderation to an end, but what followed from 2009–2020 would be the longest recorded US economic expansion. It was only finally stopped in its tracks by the arrival of COVID-19 in early 2020, a pandemic which triggered previously unimaginable lockdowns and restrictions on individual liberty.

This may be because The Great Moderation was the ideal backdrop for a series of transformative but contentious and disruptive technological innovations that would completely change the economy. These forced the pace of globalisation and saw whole sectors reconstruct themselves at warp speed. In different political circumstances there might have been far more resistance to the rise of a small set of essentially American technology companies to become such important international actors.

This was the order in which almost all of those who are senior leaders right now, be it heading listed companies, private businesses, the professional services, the public sector, or not-for-profit entities, cut their teeth and established their credentials. It allowed them to make (often unacknowledged) assumptions which were critical to the direction in which they were able to take their organisations. It placed parameters around what was and was not plausible in terms of domestic politics and policy and how nations would or would not interact with each other. It was an arrangement that placed a high premium on being an 'insider', a figure convinced of and comfortable with this consensus, and it kept its critics, who would inevitably by the very fact of their dissent be outsiders, well in the cold.

The Great Moderation is now no longer with us, and it is extremely unlikely to return. It has been undermined by the increasing influence of populist politics in a wide assortment of countries, by the intense impact of a pandemic that still has many more years to pass before we understand in full how much it has recast society and thus the economy, and then Russia's invasion of Ukraine. This has not only reignited inflation, disrupted supply lines of sizeable importance and sparked an energy supply crisis on an epic scale but is a repudiation of the international order of the 1990–2015 period. To some, it is also a dress rehearsal for a world in which the US and China become open adversaries.

This is where we are today, in the early stages of what I would call The Great Fragmentation. We can see what is falling apart – the undisputed dominance of the US as an international actor, the ability of central banks to becalm inflation and the strength of accelerating free trade as a doctrine. What is much harder to anticipate is whether The Great Fragmentation is itself the new world order, or if it is instead merely an interim interlude before an entirely novel geopolitical system takes its place.

All of this matters massively to anyone aspiring to lead an organisation of whatever form. It means that risk has to be reassessed radically, as what was recorded in registers past is rendered redundant. It obliges Chairs and CEOs to ask in advance, anticipate and adjust to what could be coming at them. Strategies that include only internal sectoral metrics will be akin to holding a sword without a shield.

The last decade of The Great Moderation witnessed the rise of a new term and mission in the form of ESG (Environmental, Social and Governance factors). This was a rational response to an evolving compelling demand for a responsible economics. The remainder of the 2020s and beyond will be about a new, second, ESG, the capacity to control for Events, Shocks and Geopolitics. Most organisations today are not even at Square One on this matter. They are not remotely proactive. Indeed, they struggle to be sufficiently reactive. They are stuck at Square Zero. They are clinging to the familiar characteristics of The Great Moderation for comfort. They need to see The Great Fragmentation for what it is and react to it. This is an age of adapt or die.

In retrospect, the final term of Barack Obama as the President of the United States was the last hurrah for an age that had started when he was a very young man, and when the notion that an individual with his background might become the most powerful man in the world would have been somewhat far-fetched. There was by 2016 sufficient dissatisfaction with what had become the new order that Mr Trump could secure the Republican nomination and then (in the electoral college if not the popular vote) defeat Hillary Clinton, a woman who personified The Great Moderation Party and the establishment worldview, and enter the Oval Office in what seemed a shocking triumph. It is hard to believe that this would have happened had not The Great Fragmentation started to emerge.

The problem for President Trump in his first term of office was that although The Great Fragmentation had propelled him into the Oval Office, he was now the one riding the tiger. It was not merely the unexpected nature of his victory,

the often chaotic means by which his Administration oper-
ated and, ultimately, the thunderbolt of a coronavirus which
undermined what might have been, despite all of the turbulence associated with his tenure, a successful re-election bid
based on a highly resilient US economy; particularly if, as
seemed very possible in early 2020, Senator Bernie Sanders
of Vermont had snatched the Democratic Party nomination
(which would have been a coup d'état on a scale to rival the
Trump takeover of the Republicans: Mr Trump was at least a
registered Republican; Mr Sanders is an independent except
when he wished to be the Democratic contender for President). In November 2020, in the very odd conditions of that
American election, Mr Trump would be ousted. His camp
did not understand The Great Fragmentation either.

This was not the case in 2024; the battle-lines would be
drawn much more sharply and clearly. It made little difference in this respect when President Biden stood down for
Vice President Harris.

In terms of basic outlook on the international arena, any
Democratic presidential contender (assuming that Senator
Sanders is no longer under consideration) would be more predictable – actually considerably more predictable – on foreign
policy and international economics than Mr Trump. This is
because there is a high level of consensus among its elites
within the Democratic Party as to how US foreign policy
should be conducted. In the past thirty or so years there have
been three Democratic presidencies, and the continuity in
ethos and policy towards international affairs between the
Clinton Administration (after a rather rocky start), the Obama
Administration and the Biden Administration is striking and
contrasts with the much more diverse instincts on foreign
policy between George H. W. Bush, George W. Bush and
Donald Trump. The core points on which the vast majority

of senior Democrats view the interaction of the United States with the outside world are:

- It is right, proper and indeed inevitable that the United States will be the world leader. It is the first obligation of any occupant of the White House to seek to retain this situation.
- The political strength of the United States is and can only be maintained by its economic strength which is best secured by multilateral co-operation (and usually free trade).
- The United States has its own national interests to protect but also has national values. There are times when pure national interest should be subordinated to those national values.
- Democracy and human rights should be a significant factor in foreign policy decisions.
- The US can operate on its own, if it wishes, but it is preferable to do this with its allies. This is partly a matter of simple practicality but also because it confers additional legitimacy.
- Transnational institutions, be they political, economic or military, are very important.
- A strong military is a crucial deterrent, but the use of force is a last, rarely a first, resort.
- The concept of 'soft power' (widespread cultural influence) is highly consequential.
- The intelligent application of economic inducements and sanctions can be very effective.
- All of the above is enhanced by achieving bipartisanship in articulating US foreign policy.

It is no exaggeration to state that at least 80% of Democratic elites would agree with more than 80% of the list just outlined (one admittedly devised by this author) more than 80% of the time.

Any Harris Administration would have accepted these ten key assertions.

Which is very comforting for European political elites and those in East Asia who think similarly. It does not ensure harmony between the United States and China, but it does make it possible to establish the outlines of a relationship which involves considerable competition in some spheres while allowing for co-operation and collaboration elsewhere and strenuously avoiding overt conflict.

There is, however, one extremely large elephant (or should that be a donkey?) trap here. These fundamental principles upon which almost any mainstream Democrat would construct their approach to foreign policy, and also to international economics, were framed in the age of The Great Moderation and have barely been adjusted to deal with the new realities of The Great Fragmentation. The only one of them which has frayed has been the firm faith in free trade, particularly when it comes to the United States and China, although establishment Democrats often regret this fissure emerging.

There is the very real risk that attempting to function on the basis of the principles of the past will prove ineffective in the present. The State Department of a Harris Administration might have found itself attempting to do its business on the Highway Code when road rage has become established as the new normal. Put another way, it may be like following the instructions for the operation of a vacuum cleaner when a chainsaw is the instrument to be handled. Put more prosaically it might be akin to speaking Ancient Greek in a world newly dominated by Ancient Rome. This was seen under the Biden Administration which looked like a spectator in the

Middle East after Israel decided to take the fight to its foes full-on in Autumn 2024.

At the 2024 election it was evident that Mr Trump had rejected the ten principles for engagement in the world in a much more holistic sense than he did in 2016, and that a large section of the American people shared his scepticism about them. In 2016 he mostly had slogans. He did not have a strategy. Whether overtly stated or not, his was a candidacy that was framed by The Great Fragmentation.

To run through the list above, which his Democratic rival would have embraced unambiguously:

- Mr Trump does not think that global leadership is an obligation that is 'right, proper and indeed inevitable' for the United States, but is instead one where a form of cost-benefit analysis is right.
- The political strength of the United States might well, the Trump contingent would acknowledge, need to be maintained by its economic strength but that economic dominance is highly desirable irrespective of the political strength it might create and is not contingent on multi-level collaboration and emphatically not on free trade. The US should instead reinforce its might by active tariff policies.
- The United States has its national interests to protect. They supersede any notion of national values. The idea of compromising or sacrificing national interests for national values is deeply unattractive.
- Democracy and human rights should not, therefore, be a significant consideration in foreign policy.
- The US most certainly can operate on its own if it so wishes and others are welcome to follow its lead but there is no particular preference for collaborating with

allies unless this is a cost saving. Even here, it should not require the United States to dilute its choice of action to obtain allies' approval.

- Transnational institutions – political, economic or military – are rarely to be thought very important.
- A strong military is a crucial deterrent, and the use of force can be a first resort if that is effective.
- The concept of 'soft power' (widespread cultural influence) is all too frequently exaggerated.
- The intelligent application of economic inducements and sanctions are only likely to be effective if imposed on such a scale as to force the hand of those whom they are being directed against.
- There is no shining virtue in achieving bipartisanship in American foreign policy just for its own sake. Splitting the difference between Republicans and Democrats might well be the worst of approaches.

The divisions between Mr Trump and Mrs Clinton in 2016 or between then President Trump and the then ex-Vice President Biden in 2020, were nothing like as profound as the chasm which existed between then former President Trump and first President Biden and then Vice President Harris in 2024. That battle was the first that might properly be described as a Great Fragmentation political contest. It was the moment when the age of The Great Moderation finally exited history. The contrast in outlooks was far more fundamental in terms of foreign policy than domestic issues.

In all of this one essential message should be remembered, especially by those who might find the implicit disruption that I have set out disturbing (to put it mildly). Donald Trump did not create The Great Fragmentation. The Great

Fragmentation enabled Donald Trump to be a viable political figure. This is hardly unique to the United States. The same sorts of forces have been seen in the stunning political volatility of late in the UK, or in France, Germany, Italy, the Netherlands and in Austria. It has made being an incumbent administration a potential poisoned chalice almost universally. It is simply that the sheer size of the United States makes it more visible and much more consequential.

It is, in short, impossible to comprehend the initial rise and now return of Mr Trump without a full consideration of how much has changed since the previous Republican to serve as President stood down in 2008 (George W. Bush), let alone the one defeated as he sought his second term in 1992 (George H. W. Bush). The Great Fragmentation is the new order. Mr Trump is its logical outcome.

CHAPTER THREE

FIRST TERM

An unconventional President finds himself the apprentice in the White House

The consensus conclusion about the first Trump term in office is that it was a time of chaos and extreme controversy, leading to a highly predictable defeat (if narrow in the states which would prove critical in the electoral college), and what was left of any favourable assessment deleted entirely by his refusal to admit that Joe Biden had beaten him and the events of 6 January 2021. On that basis, the suggestion that he might obtain a second term in 2025 would seem insane.

This is, though, exactly the position that the American political establishment finds itself in.

It would be hard to deny some truth (probably considerable legitimacy) to the charge of chaos and extreme controversy. What is required, however, is some context as to why this occurred.

Mr Trump descended from Trump Tower in New York in June 2015 to make his declaration for the presidency. Many took this to be little more than a publicity stunt (*The Apprentice* had just about run its course) and as he had hinted at such a course of action before but then abandoned it, a lot of political observers doubted whether he would see his pledge through. If he did, almost all of them concurred, then while he might start as the front-runner due to his name recognition, once the extremely large field winnowed after the opening caucuses and primaries, then the figure who emerged as the 'Not Trump' choice would surely draw a majority to his standard. If somehow that did not materialise, then he would be derailed by Hillary Clinton on election day. The smart money was on Jeb Bush, not Mr Trump, to be the next Republican President. The former Governor of Florida had lined up most of the ducks that a victor normally needed.

After all, Mr Trump had little more than a slogan ('Make American Great Again', which would obtain all but 100% recognition) and later 'drain the swamp' and 'lock her up'. That was not enough, surely?

As matters evolved this analysis proved almost entirely mistaken. He did not crash out of the race early. Mr Bush was to suffer that fate. His electoral excursion had a slightly shaky start in the Iowa caucuses where he came in behind Senator Ted Cruz by a handy margin and almost fell to third after Senator Marco Rubio, who produced a strong late showing, but it was an OK result. Mr Trump romped home in the New Hampshire Primary and breezed into first place in the South Carolina Primary thereafter (with the conspicuous exception of 2012, when the Republicans in that state backed Newt Gingrich over Mitt Romney, it has been a reliable indicator of whom the nominee would turn out to be). A further triumph in Florida and a sweep on Super Tuesday led most of his opponents to abandon the contest, lick their wounds and reluctantly endorse him. Only John Kasich, the former Governor of Ohio, wanted to carry on, but he was a doomed figure.

This was only the first phase of the battle. The Republican Convention was a strange affair as the Trump family would lean into the limelight but also reveal their political inexperience. The selection of Governor Mike Pence of Indiana reassured social and religious conservatives (not that a large number of orthodox electoral officials were desperate for inclusion on the ticket). There was a minor flap over whether Mrs Trump (or to be more accurate her speechwriter) had borrowed too shamelessly from the words that Michelle Obama had delivered four years before. It did not have the feel of a candidacy that was on the verge of usurping Hillary Clinton's ambitions.

The sentiment that she was the clear favourite continued over the next few months, but at no stage did she sustain a substantial lead over her insurgent opponent. She had an awkward moment when she appeared to faint, or worse still collapse, while returning to an automobile. The claims and counterclaims about her alleged misuse of personal email facilities while she had been the Secretary of State in the first Obama Administration would not disappear either. Nor was the departing President wildly popular and her relationship with him often struck others as frigid.

She remained the favourite. If there was a 'health issue' it did not hang over her excessively. She was seen to have performed competently in the three raucous debates that were conducted. When a tape emerged (from a decade earlier) of Mr Trump discussing his techniques in dealing with women, including the infamous 'grab them by the pussy' observation, the Democrat looked as if she was home and dry, while Republicans asked themselves if Mr Trump should be forced to stand down and let Mr Pence attempt to minimise the scale of the apparently imminent loss. Mr Trump held his ground. The polls narrowed once more, but with Mrs Clinton always ahead. On the morning of the election the betting odds were more than 80% in her favour. She would have been more than entitled to spend that day writing down what would be a savoured victory speech.

The words would never pass her lips. By the early morning

afterwards it was evident that Mr Trump had pulled off an unanticipated upset. Mrs Clinton probably demeaned her own status by not conceding more swiftly than she did. There were tears aplenty inside the inner Trump family, but whether because he had won or for his failure to be defeated as expected is not certain.

What is clear is that, insofar as there was a transition team doing business for Mr Trump, it had not made it to first base yet. There was (in the circumstances) an amicable enough meeting held between the President-Elect and the soon to be ex-President Obama, but this could not serve as a substitute for a more orderly process of preparing for the most awesome of responsibilities. The Republican leadership in Congress had little sense of what to prepare for either and found that their President in waiting had a semi-detached approach towards them. Absolutely no one – including the new occupant of the Oval Office – really knew what would happen once he was in.

There is a further factor to consider here. In a structure championed by this author, incoming Presidents fall into three categories. The first are those who not only win election themselves but also see their party retake one or both chambers of Congress. This happened with Dwight D. Eisenhower in 1953 (both the Senate and the House), Ronald Reagan in 1981 (the Republicans seized the Senate and the new President had de facto control of the House for many of his key domestic priorities) and Joe Biden in 2021 (with the Senate falling to the Democrats). This adds to a sense of momentum and assists legislative success. Many Presidents are in Category B. They inherit existing congressional majorities. This was true for Harry Truman on the death of FDR in 1945, John F. Kennedy in 1961, Lyndon Johnson on Kennedy's assassination in 1963, Jimmy Carter in 1977, Bill Clinton in 1993, George W. Bush in 2001 (although a defection meant that he lost command of the Senate after four months) and Barack Obama in 2009. This is a decent place to be in politically but not as dominant as a Category A President has the chance to be. Finally, there are those who become President bereft of a majority in either segment of Congress (such as Richard Nixon in 1969, Gerald Ford in 1974 and George H. W. Bush in 1989). In domestic political terms, this is a weak hand (and none of these three men would serve a full second term). To make matters worse for the occupant of the Oval Office, mid-term election losses can move them partly or fully into the Category C space – Mr Eisenhower (1955-1961), Mr Reagan (1987-1989), Mr Clinton (1995-2001), Mr Bush (2001-2003 in the Senate, 2007-2009 for the whole of Congress), Mr Obama (2011-2015 in the House, 2015-2017 for all Congress) would all share that fate and be forced to recast their political ambitions as a consequence.

Mr Trump thus started as a Category B President with the risk of becoming a Category C one after the 2018 mid-term elections. That would have mattered even if he had been far better prepared for the assumption of power than would very quickly become clear that he was not.

The chaos was baked in before the Oath of Office was administered. The key appointments to the White House staff, to the Cabinet and elsewhere were an uneasy mixture of a few people whom Mr Trump knew well personally and others who had been recommended to him by his adopted party, but often on the basis that they would be a constraint on his personal instincts. All of this made turbulence unavoidable. It was signalled by an uncompromising Inauguration Address in which Mr Trump revisited campaign slogans and spoke of an 'American carnage'. After he had finished orating, former President George W. Bush supposedly turned to Mrs Clinton and asked the rhetorical question 'what was all that sh*t about?' An unedifying row as to the size of the crowd that attended the event promptly followed and the interesting concept of 'alternative facts' was floated by the President's principal media spokesperson.

So, the first eighteen months of the Trump Administration were unambiguously chaotic. An unprecedented turnover rate approaching 50% was witnessed during this time. The first National Security Adviser was fired within a month for misleading Vice President Pence about the extent of his (Michael Flynn's) contacts with the Russian Ambassador before the election. The opening Chief of Staff, former RNC Chair Reince Priebus, lasted scarcely six months to be replaced by John Kelly (who would in 2024 label his former boss a fascist and endorse his rival). The opening Secretary of State, Rex Tillerson, who had been a corporate king at Exxon before, was fired by tweet after a year in post and supplanted by Mike Pompeo, then the CIA Director. There would be many other examples of Mr Trump doubting the loyalties of those around him. One of the most incendiary incidents came with the dismissal of FBI Director James Comey. Within the White House staff, Steve Bannon came and went as did a set of Press Secretaries. It may have been in the spirit of *The Apprentice* to say 'you're fired', but who would be left?

The cascade of controversies during and after this time was to become an extraordinary torrent. Some of them could and should have been avoided. Mr Trump's choice of words in condemning violence on 'many sides' after an outrage in Charlottesville, Virginia when a collection of white nationalists and supremacists provoked a de facto riot which involved a woman being killed when a neo-Nazi sympathiser drove into a crowd of counter-protestors, was very poorly judged. His response three years later to the death of George Floyd in Minnesota indicated that he was rather less bothered about the video showing appalling police brutality than in responding to rioting or looting by the swift deployment of live ammunition against any of those who protested. The endless barrage of tweets which emerged from his own account rather than the formal Oval Office diminished the dignity of the presidency. There were many times when Washington asked itself whether anyone was in any sort of charge.

There were additional episodes which imperilled Mr Trump's tenure directly. He had been dogged by the allegation that not only had Russia intervened in the election to his aid but that those around him (perhaps Mr Trump as well) knew of this and were relaxed about it. Jeff Sessions, his first Attorney General, decided to appoint Robert Mueller as a Special Counsel to investigate the assertion (he would soon be dismissed by the President for this decision). In the end, Mr Mueller's report found that while Russia had certainly been active in attempting to undermine US democracy, the suggestion of outright collusion with Team Trump lacked proof. This was far from a vindication of the President, but it did not stop his allies insisting that it was.

The White House would instead move out of the Russian frying pan into the Ukrainian fire. It became clear that Mr Trump had in telephone calls to President Zelensky sought to pressure him to announce investigations into the role of ex-Vice President Joe Biden and his wayward son Hunter involving corrupt commercial engagement in Kyiv, with the firm hint that US assistance to Ukraine would be contingent on such an initiative being realised. There were serious reasons to probe why Mr Biden senior had chosen to involve himself in the affairs of Ukraine as a Special Envoy and what on Earth Hunter Biden did in return for his significant financial rewards from what appeared to be rather mysterious and obscure business associates in Ukraine, but Mr Trump should not have been involved here.

The result was that the Democrats, who had retaken the House of Representatives in some style in the mid-term elections of November 2018, took their chance to move against the President. He was subjected to an impeachment vote which was carried in the House in late December 2019, although all those involved were aware that it would not be sustained in the Senate (where it was lost on an almost totally party-line vote in February 2020). It was a shot across the bows. It was designed to put the Administration right on the defensive in its re-election year.

So, neither chaos nor controversy can be disregarded as hyperbole. The more important issue with respect to the return of Mr Trump to the presidency is whether they are certain to be repeated once again simply because of the nature of his character, or whether they were to a sizeable degree the consequence of the exceptional conditions of his initial time in office. Will he benefit from being much more experienced at the second time of asking? If not exactly a more mellow individual after a break of four years, might he be a more careful political figure? If he has a White House staff and a Cabinet in which he has trust, will he be far more contented? In practice, the only way to find out is to live with the restored Trump presidency as it happens.

What in policy terms was the original Trump tenure like, particularly as he became established?

In domestic policy, while he was an unconventional President he was not a deviant Republican.

His signature legislative accomplishment was the Tax Cuts and Jobs Act, which was enacted in December 2017 after the feuding Republican factions in Congress finally united behind it. This was a landmark measure with a major impact on US fiscal policy for years to come (but with a number of central provisions subject to a sunset clause in 2025 if not endorsed once more). There was more than a touch of Ronald Reagan to this Act but with large cuts in Corporation Tax (from 35% to 21%) as a key plank and a series of measures which reduced personal taxes as well. There were some quirks reflecting his own sense of economic priorities, but this was well within Republican orthodox thinking.

This was the case across numerous fronts, especially when the Republicans held the House of Representatives and the Senate as they did from 2017–2019 (the atmosphere when Nancy Pelosi was returned to be the Speaker of the House at the helm of the Democrats after 2019 was a different state of affairs altogether). As President, Mr Trump sought to repeal the Affordable Healthcare Act (or 'Obamacare') as virtually all Republican contenders had promised to do in the 2016 presidential election, but fell short when his nemesis John McCain declined to back its abolition without a coherent alternative being offered in its place in a dramatic moment on the Senate floor (the pivotal individual mandate provision within it was gutted in the details of the Tax Cuts and Jobs Act a few months later). The Administration led the charge for deregulation in many sectors but was devoted with special force to reversing environmental regulations that the Obama White House had supported. This was once again a standard Republican position. The President signed the Great American Outdoors Act, which encouraged traditional conservation.

Mr Trump attempted repeatedly to extract much more money from Congress to enable him to complete the kind of border wall with Mexico which he had long been the cheerleader for and was willing to accept the longest US federal government shutdown in history as a means to that end. He did not get his way and had to look to the equivalent of sticking-plaster solutions to add to border security. Another Republican President might have been less insistent on this point, but it had been a central message of his campaign in 2016 and was not out of the mainstream. In a string of other instances, Mr Trump at home was not that far from Republican orthodoxy.

This included his approach towards the federal judiciary, which delighted the conservatives. He made three appointments to the Supreme Court, namely Neil Gorsuch, Brett Kavanaugh and in the last weeks before the 2020 election, the seminal selection of Amy Coney Barrett, who would tip the Court towards a decisive and stable 6–3 majority on most social decisions. While Mr Kavanaugh had a very awkward confirmation hearing when accusations of a college-era rape incident were made against him, in all other respects these were people with strong qualifications to be placed on the Court and whom George W. Bush (or a theoretical President Ted Cruz, President Marco Rubio or even a President John Kasich) would not have been troubled by nominating. At a lower level, Mr Trump saw 260 of his choices for federal judges confirmed, with the distinctive feature that a third of them were under the age of 45 so could be in situ for decades. This was part of a conservative strategy for reshaping the judiciary that was not his invention but which he implemented for that movement.

In summary, despite the chaos and controversies, at home President Trump was not abnormal.

Where he did behave as other Republican Presidents would not have done was in foreign policy and international economics. The list of Trumpian activities here is extensive. In his first term he withdrew from the Paris Agreement on Climate Change, abandoned negotiations over the Trans-Pacific Partnership, similarly sunk the EU Transatlantic Trade and Investment Partnership, insisted on replacing the North American Free Trade Agreement, which had been adopted back in 1993 by President Clinton with the favour of the congressional Republican hierarchy, with his own bespoke US-Mexico-Canada Agreement (how different this was can be argued about) and in the last gasp of his first term tried to pull the US out of the World Health Organization (the Biden Administration was able to pull the brake on this announcement). Multilateralism in many forms (which past US Republican Presidents had often been pioneers of) was out of fashion. He held NATO in open contempt (having previously dubbed it 'obsolete' on the campaign trail).

There are many other examples of the Trump Effect being most marked abroad during his first term of office. He was enchanted by the adversarial use of tariffs, initially in fairly boutique sectors such as solar panels and washing machines but then with more serious items such as steel and aluminium. Allies such as the EU, Canada and Mexico were all in the firing line. A much more fundamental deployment of tariffs was aimed at the economic rise of China and its exports to the United States with a 'trade war' from 2018. It is challenging to conceive that a more mainstream Republican President would have done this. Mr Trump tended to be softer on Russia as it was not seen as an economic competitor to the US, although he was very unimpressed by the willingness of Germany to depend on Russian gas (he turned out to be ahead of the field on that one). He would reluctantly show up at G7 summits but made it clear that he did not see them as having any right to limit his own economic options.

The Trump earthquake was felt the strongest in East Asia and the Middle East. He became an adversary of China (while sometimes praising its President for his defence of its interests) and spent an exceptional amount of time on his dialogue with Kim Jong Un of North Korea (no other Republican would have volunteered to meet with him once, never mind on three occasions). It led nowhere but it drove South Korea and Japan to distraction (although in the latter case, the then Prime Minister Shinzo Abe managed to be on excellent terms with Mr Trump regardless. A mutual passion for playing golf may have helped).

In the Middle East, the impact of President Trump was seismic. It had been a ritual that almost all presidential aspirants stated while seeking votes that they would recognise Jerusalem as the capital of Israel and then reconsidered that stance once in the Oval Office. Mr Trump did do it. He also favoured a major arms sale to Saudi Arabia and was the catalyst for the Abraham Accords which allowed Israel and a set of Gulf States to come to terms with each other (as a diplomatic initiative it could be considered the American achievement of the decade). He took US troops out of northern Syria (and sent the green light to Turkey to move its own soldiers in). He had little time for the squabbling communities within Iraq. He reached a tentative deal with the Taliban in Afghanistan to take the US military out of that country (but would condemn President Biden later when he implemented this). He was much more assertive towards Iran, repudiating the bargain that had been struck with its leadership to restrict their drive to become a nuclear weapons state and in a stunning move ordering a drone strike to kill Qasem Soleimani in early 2020. Travel bans on citizens of various Muslim-majority nations were imposed as well.

The first Trump term should – whether one favours it or not – be thought of as a radical, in some places almost revolutionary, development in foreign policy and international economics. One does not have to be a policy detective of the highest calibre to look for clues as to what might be the biggest effect of his return to the Oval Office. It will be far from the shores of the US itself. Although many of his decisions were contentious, they did have an internal coherence to them. The first term suggested a view of the world which was more than a fickle or fragile fascination.

When he entered 2020 (apart from the inconvenience of fending off impeachment), Mr Trump's prospects for re-election were, while on balance uneasy, not an incredible proposition. There was more stability within his Administration. He would not face a threat in the primaries. His party appreciated that its fate was inextricably tied to that of the President. The economy was in reasonable shape. His approval ratings in the early months of that year touched 49% which was the best that he had recorded in office. The set of prospective Democratic opponents was not that intimidating. If there was a frontrunner it was Senator Bernie Sanders of Vermont, who would not sue if it were suggested that he was a socialist. For all of the chaos and the immense controversy, there were many seasoned observers of US politics who saw another Trump win coming.

And then came COVID-19, which would change the picture entirely. The President was slow to accept the scale of the pandemic, the number of deaths which would materialise if draconian measures were not accepted and was not remotely keen on shuttering the US economy. The American reaction to COVID-19 was thus haphazard and it varied across state lines drastically. The President made some wise calls, throwing his weight behind 'Operation Warp Speed', the quest to find a vaccine in record time, even if Moderna and not Pfizer was the preference. As the coronavirus closed in, the Democrat contest moved towards ex-Vice President Biden. The campaign was all but suspended due to the restrictions introduced. The national conventions were not conducted as would have been expected. The contest that followed did not involve the normal route either, which allowed Mr Biden to stay based in Delaware and not have his mental and physical state tested in the intrusive heat of the campaign trail. Above all else, the economy, in fine fettle until the virus took hold, would enter into a recession.

This combination of conditions would curtail the Trump tenure in Washington. There were some embarrassingly ugly debates between the two contenders, but it was not electoral politics as usual. There was a new contingent of discontented voters for the Democrats to find and mine. In many states, out of necessity as it was perceived, the arrangements surrounding voting by mail were eased significantly, a switch that the Democrats made the most of, while the Trump campaign, even before the election day itself, was denouncing this as distorting democracy.

This set the scene for the endgame. Once again, the opinion polls understated Mr Trump and implied that his Democratic rival would defeat him by a convincing margin. Mr Biden was a shade over 4% ahead in the popular vote (about double the edge that Mrs Clinton managed) but squeaked home in the electoral college courtesy of Arizona, Georgia, Michigan, Pennsylvania and Wisconsin. It would be Saturday afternoon, after the Tuesday election day itself, before victory was there.

The Trump first term finished in a torrid climax. It was bad enough that he did not concede defeat, attempted to twist the arm of Vice President Pence not to confirm the result and was at best agnostic when a demonstration in his favour in Washington morphed into an uprising. The spectacle was atrocious. A (pointless) second impeachment attempt was then launched. It would be voted on in the Senate only after Mr Trump had departed from the capital city, having refused to attend the inauguration of his successor. The end was a return to the chaos that had been the hallmark of much of the first half of his tenure. Surely, there was no way back for him.

CHAPTER FOUR

THE CORONATION NOMINATION

*How Donald Trump secured the support of the
Republican Party once again*

The early stages of Donald Trump's enforced political retirement were those of discontent. The sense of them is
captured in a *New York Times* article of 7 November 2024
('Pariah, felon, president-elect: How he did it' by Matt
Flegenheimer, Maggie Haberman, Jonathan Swan).

By late January 2021, just days into Donald Trump's
unhappy new life as a former president, his world had
shrunk to a size he could not abide.

Self-exiled in Florida as a twice-impeached, semi-pari-
ah, he golfed and glowered, boiling over his 2020 defeat
and still refusing to acknowledge its legitimacy. His social
media bullhorns had been silenced after Jan 6, 2021, with
Twitter citing 'the risk of further incitement of violence'.
His circle had dwindled to a smattering of junior aides,
straining to keep him on the fairways and away from the
television.

'Get the pool,' Mr Trump instructed at one point, refer-
ring to the hive of reporters who had trailed him daily as
president. 'I want to make a statement.' He was told that
he did not have one anymore.

By late February, Mr Trump had waited long enough.
In his first public appearance as a newly private citizen,

he accepted an invitation to Orlando for a conference of right-wing activists.

'Do you miss me yet?' he asked, his arms splayed wide as if waiting to be hugged.

It had been five weeks. Outside of that room, most Americans did not seem to miss him much at all.

All the indicators are that Mr Trump had decided upon his political comeback almost instantly. He would be launching what would be, in effect, the longest presidential campaign in history (and there is no shortage of contenders for that accolade). It did not look like a promising plan. By June 2021, he had started a series of campaign-like rallies. The crowds were respectable in size but not on the scale that he had attracted in 2015–2016 or when he was in the Oval Office. There was an element of nostalgia about the entire exercise, akin to an ageing rock star belting out his old hits to the faithful but with little prospect of sitting atop the charts once again.

It was also a phony war. There was a very long time to wait, and conventional wisdom was that time was not on Mr Trump's side. The calendar would allow other candidates the room to grow. The number of devoted Republicans who ached for a Trump-Biden rematch was not impressive.

There was a small shift in gear as 2022 arrived. In the February of that year Mr Trump came out on top of a straw poll at the Conservative Political Action Committee conference and did so by a thirty-point margin. He still had a base within his party, but how firm it was would be tested. In March, he said that, if he did stand again, Mike Pence would not be his vice-presidential running mate (this can hardly have been news to Mr Pence, and if it were then it was not unwelcome). In July he stated in an interview that he had already decided to run again. The only issue was if he should formally announce before the mid-term elections or after them (the congressional GOP was desperate for him to defer lest his entering the race earlier put off some potential voters).

There was a strategy at work here. It was an attempt to make his return appear inevitable and deter other aspirants for the White House from committing themselves to the contest, or if they had the temerity to do so to cut off their chances of raising sufficient funds to take him on.

What was to become a menace was the sheer range of legal obstacles he might encounter. In August, the FBI obtained a search warrant for his Mar-a-Lago estate in pursuit of any official documents that might have been misplaced there. They came out with a small treasure trove.

A period of relative peace on the presidential front then occurred as the Republicans focused on the November elections, where past form suggested that they had a strong chance of seizing the House of Representatives and a decent prospect of making the net gain of just one seat in the Senate which would put them in control there as well. A double win would badly hurt Joe Biden. Mr Trump did his duty on the campaign trail and more or less avoided promoting himself over the congressional Republican whom he was meant to be championing. He could not resist a more active role despite this. He took delight in endorsing personal loyalists in critical Senate races in states such as Arizona and Pennsylvania, and he made every effort to turbocharge his supporters to vote against those Republican members of the House of Representatives who had backed the second impeachment initiative against him when they sought primary renomination.

The outcome of those elections was a low point for Project Trump Restoration. There had been much chatter in Republican circles and more neutral camps that 2022 would bring in a 'red wave' in the House of Representatives, a landslide of the type that had been recorded against Bill Clinton in 1994 and Barack Obama in 2010. An advance of 40 seats or more looked possible. When the returns came in, it was rather more akin to a 'red puddle' than any 'red wave'. The Republicans had retaken the House but with a net switch of a meagre nine seats in their favour. Furthermore, it was clear that the disappointed and surly caucus would not allow its putative leader, Kevin McCarthy, to take up the position of Speaker without public attempts to block him. Mr Trump was left in a very inconvenient place and uncharacteristically silent on the fratricide.

It was worse still in the Senate. The Republicans not only failed to snatch that chamber back, the Democrats obtained an improbable additional seat via a win in Pennsylvania. This had not been expected. Blame was placed firmly on Mr Trump for wading in on behalf of his people in the critical states without regard to the fact that they were politically inexperienced and/or seen as extremists. Most of them, like the ex-President himself, continued to insist that the 2020 presidential result was suspect. One of the few who did prevail was a Mr J. D. Vance in Ohio.

The most damaging aspect of the entire episode was not a Republican defeat but a victory. Ron DeSantis, the Governor of Florida, secured re-election by an unexpectedly emphatic margin. He was much younger than Mr Trump, had impeccable conservative credentials of his own and he had none of the baggage of the former President. In late 2022, DeSantis looked like DeFuture. Many of the most important donors and Republican-inclined media figures moved towards him.

Mr Trump did not want to allow that bandwagon to acquire any more momentum. The Governor could not really announce that he was standing for President when he had not even been sworn in for the second time for the office that he currently held and had been re-elected for. It made sense for Mr Trump to move first. He officially declared for the presidency on 15 November.

Three days later, another legal bombshell was dropped on him. Merrick Garland, the Attorney General in the Biden Administration, appointed Jack Smith, something of a terrier, to become a Special Counsel to investigate Mr Trump over his part in the US Capitol attacks on 6 January 2021, and for mishandling government documents. This was seen as a menacing moment.

It encouraged other possible Republican candidates to pursue their hopes. On 14 February, Nikki Haley, a former Governor of South Carolina who had served as the American Ambassador to the United Nations under Mr Trump, announced that she was running. On paper she was an exceptionally plausible alternative both to the ex-President and the sitting President as the Democratic nominee presumptive. She was telegenic, comparatively youthful and seen as a moderate capable of appealing to those who were not aligned to either of the major parties. For these reasons, she was also well set to win donations from several multi-millionaire donors. A week later Vivek Ramaswamy, a technology entrepreneur who was almost unknown, was in too. His assets were that he was rich enough to finance his own bid and he was fresh on the menu.

The Trump brand remained viable. In March 2023, he again stormed the Conservative Political Action Committee straw poll, this time by 42 points with Governor DeSantis in his wake.

The courtroom was a different kind of straw poll that Mr Trump could be doing without. In late March he was indicted by a Manhattan Grand Jury on multiple charges relating to the 'hush money' paid to pornography actress Stormy Daniels, said to buy her silence before the 2016 election. Two weeks later, the ex-President and presidential contender had to turn himself in at New York.

It was becoming something of a habit. In May, Mr Trump would be found guilty in a civil suit of sexually assaulting and defaming E. Jean Carroll, an author. She was awarded damages of $5 million (the sum would escalate dramatically in later proceedings). He angrily denied this.

More Republicans were polishing their hats ready to throw them in the ring. On 19 May, Senator Tim Scott of South Carolina, an amiable Black Republican of some stature, was a candidate. A few days later Ron DeSantis also declared through an interview with Elon Musk, which was plagued with technological imperfections (paradoxically as it transpired, as Mr Musk would later volunteer his weight and his wallet behind Mr Trump and forget all about the Governor). Chris Christie, the ex-Governor of New Jersey, was also in the frame by June 2023, as would be former Vice President Mike Pence and, with lesser prospects, Governor Doug Burgum of North Dakota. This was a slight to Mr Trump in that it indicated that all of these figures now thought that he could be beaten for the nomination. The plus was that it also meant that he faced divided opposition.

He had more pressing legal matters. He was indicted for the second time by Jack Smith over the files that had moved from the White House to Florida without due authorisation. He had to turn up at a federal district court in Miami to plead not guilty to 37 felony counts (in addition to the separate 34 charges in New York). By 1 August he would be indicted yet again by Mr Smith on his alleged participation in an illegal conspiracy to overturn the outcome of the 2020 election. This time the courtroom concerned was in Washington, D.C. and involved four felony counts.

This made Mr Trump even more of a target for his

Republican rivals, although they were aware that his argument that he was himself the victim of a plot to twist the law to bring him down had a substantial constituency across the Republican faithful. This sentiment was so entrenched that Mr Trump's approval rating among his party adherents appeared to rise in line with the number of charges that were being brought against him. The likes of Mr DeSantis and Ms Haley were equivocal about how to handle this. Should they urge him to withdraw from the race or would that look like they were dancing to a tune being played by prosecutors linked to the Biden Administration or the Democratic Party? After mulling the matter over, they put on kid gloves rather than the iron fist. The closest that anyone would come to denouncing Mr Trump and suggesting that there might be no smoke without fire in all these legal investigations of him was Mr Pence, but even he was unwilling to be a political suicide-bomber on the matter and, in any case, he was not viewed as entirely agnostic about Mr Trump's ethical qualities any longer. Chris Christie came out swinging at Mr Trump on other issues (it seemed to be the sole point of his run). In what was becoming a staring competition, the ex-President was never about to blink first.

Instead, he doubled down. The Republican National Committee had decided some months earlier that it would sponsor televised debates between the candidates and created a system to determine which contenders had enough support to qualify for a place at the podium. Mr Trump made it apparent that he would not share a stage with the other candidates. He had no need to do so. His views on virtually every subject under the sun were already known and besides which it was transparent from the opinion polling that the party had already decided they wanted him. It was a risky approach (smacking of arrogance) but it could take the air out of the debates (of which there would be several). Once more, his opponents failed to damn him for his decision.

That he avoided the opening debate in August 2023 was fortuitous. A few days beforehand, he was indicted (for the fourth time but all related to different legal occurrences) over his drive to overturn the election results of 2020 in Georgia (a recording of a telephone conversation existed in which he plainly pressured Governor Brian Kemp to 'find him' the votes he needed to win). This was, therefore, a state case and not a federal one. Mr Trump had to surrender to the legal authorities in Atlanta and this time endure the indignity of being finger-printed and a mug shot. For any other politician this would surely be fatal. He was turning it into his badge of honour.

An additional legal front was opened. His alleged involvement in incitement to insurrection (a violation of the XIVth Amendment to the US Constitution) led the state of Minnesota to seek to remove his name from the primary ballot there. Colorado and Maine would take the same tack. All had to desist from doing so until after the Supreme Court had reached a ruling on its validity.

But the Trump cat had considerably more than nine lives and his opponents were running out of cash. In late October 2023 Mike Pence suspended his candidacy. A month later Senator Scott, who had been fluent in the debates but never found a killer case for himself, did the same. The DeSantis camp was in severe financial distress and laying off staff members in large numbers. The opening contests of the nominating season were in sight, but the competition was absent.

At long, long last, election year 2024 arrived. The American people would be consulted on the Trump comeback proposition. Only a tiny proportion of them would matter for the nomination.

The opening fight was in Iowa, which conducts a caucus rather than a primary. This means that electors have to devote a large part of an evening to visiting an establishment (which in more rural areas could be someone's home), hear the merits of the candidates extolled and then declare their allegiance. Although the publicity around the Iowa event is enormous, turnout is not (although in the other states which employ a caucus, participation is absolutely minuscule). The premium is on organisation and acquiring the support of highly ideological Republicans. A fair-weather citizen does not involve themselves in a caucus on a freezing cold winter night. This had been a burden for Mr Trump when he first stood in the Iowa caucus back in 2016.

It would not be on 15 January 2024. He took the Iowa caucus with 51% of the votes cast. Governor DeSantis was a distant second with 21% and Nikki Haley came third on 19%.

Attention moved to New Hampshire. The DeSantis candidacy was holed below the water line. He departed from the race and embraced Mr Trump. Ms Haley was now the only real challenger to him. New Hampshire had form on backing upstart contenders who appealed to independents as well as Republican true believers. John McCain had triumphed in its primary in both 2000 and 2008. Ms Haley had the air of his heir and still had big money behind her. This would be her opportunity.

It was not to be. Mr Trump obtained more than 54% of the vote with Ms Haley at 43%. It was faintly ridiculous that the race could be over after only two small states had spoken but it was fast becoming the reality. If the ex-Governor of South Carolina could not top the poll in the next state, her own home state, then she would be toast. It was not even close. Mr Trump gained almost 60% of the ballot with his rival a shade under 40%. She was all but politically done for.

It did not take much longer for this to be evident. She did win a non-binding primary in Nevada, which the Trump team had chosen not to involve itself with (to be completely correct, she came second behind 'None of These Candidates' but claimed it as an endorsement). She would also win the Republican primary in Washington, D.C. which involves very few voters. On 4 March, the Supreme Court, unanimously, determined that only Congress could assert that a candidate had been involved in insurrection and was hence disqualified from high office, so any scheme to keep Mr Trump out of the contest anywhere was now no longer acceptable. One day later, it was Super Tuesday where Mr Trump carried every state bar Vermont (the land of Ben, Jerry and Nikki). A week or so after that the former President had accumulated the number of delegates that he needed to be nominated. The Haley candidacy was put on ice. The (many) states left to express a sentiment had no option other than to add to the Trump delegate tally. This would make for a subdued end to the primaries and a wait for the Republican convention which would not occur until mid-July. Vice presidential speculation had to fill the void.

A spectacular set of events in the course of 45 days would electrify the contest.

On 30 May, Mr Trump was sensationally found guilty on all 34 counts at his New York trial and hence was now a felon, a convicted criminal with sentencing to come at some later date (very much later as it turned out). There were plenty of experts who thought this was the end of him.

That was also a miscalculation. In an unprecedented move, the Biden campaign had insisted that the first of two presidential debates between the incumbent and his predecessor was held before either man had formally been nominated by their respective parties. The rationale, it was surmised, was that if the President had a poor showing, he would have plenty of time to recover. The second and final debate would follow in September, a schedule that was also a safety valve.

If the choice of 27 June 2024 for an encounter held in Atlanta was designed to be a political parachute for the President, then someone had cut the strings before he leapt from the skies. It was a 24-carat catastrophe for Mr Biden and the Democratic Party. He was so dire in the first twenty minutes that even committed partisans on his own side had to admit that he came over as close to senile. He improved (slightly) as the back-and-forth continued but still lapsed into episodes of total incoherence. All Mr Trump had to do was remain standing up and convey the capacity to count from one to ten to come over as the more lucid individual. His own rambling monologues were comparative eloquence. A convict looked preferable to a mentally defective candidate.

Mr Trump was on a roll, even if it was mostly due to Mr Biden's astonishing performance. His own party privately, but increasingly publicly, asked if the President could continue to stand for a second term at the end of which he would be 86 years old. Mr Trump's ethics issues seemed less of a controversy than whether Mr Biden had lost his marbles. Despondent Republicans perked up.

The ex-President would be boosted further when the Supreme Court on 1 July and by a 6–3 margin reached its conclusion on the extent to which he had immunity for his actions when in office. To a substantial degree, it ruled in his favour. Although the opinion was quite complex and the language chosen to support it capable of more than one interpretation, in essence the Court considered that he had absolute immunity for the official actions he committed as President within his constitutional purview. This did not in itself rescue him from his New York legal saga (the payment of $130,000 to Ms Daniels predated him entering the White House) but depending on what one took the terms 'official actions' and 'his constitutional purview' to mean, it could be treated as (literally) a 'Get Out of Jail Free' card when it came to the other cases against him.

This was not the last act in this seven-week production. The next scene was at a campaign rally in Butler, Pennsylvania on Saturday 13 July, only two days before the Republican National Convention was set to open in Milwaukee, Wisconsin.

The event started a little late but there was a sizeable audience. Mr Trump had scarcely got into his rhetorical stride when shots were directed at him from relatively close range from an AR-15-style rifle in the hands of Thomas Matthew Crooks, a 20-year-old from Bethel Park who had perched himself on a rooftop with a clear sight of his target. He had been spotted climbing up but in a slapstick series of lapses the local police and the secret service had not disabled him. He was able to fire off eight rounds before being shot dead himself. Mr Trump was staggeringly lucky to avoid a bullet to the head; he had his ear singed and he ducked to avoid worse. Agents bundled him off stage but not before a blood-streaked ex-President had defiantly raised up his fist and urged those watching him to 'fight, fight, fight'. An observer in the crowd, Corey Comperatore from Sarver, Pennsylvania, was killed trying to protect his family. There were a number of others wounded. It was all transmitted live on television.

The reaction to this stunning set of images was varied. Republicans accused Democrats of fostering an atmosphere of hate towards Mr Trump and for a while the political discourse about him did cool (the truce did not endure that long). Christian supporters of the ex-President took his survival to be evidence of divine intervention and of heavenly approval for his re-election. Conspiracy theorists muttered that the whole thing must have been staged. Very few would dispute the conclusion that Mr Trump was the stronger for his reaction. His roll rolled further.

When the Republican National Convention did start on the Monday afterwards, Mr Trump went on stage as a conquering hero. He had bandaged his ear (many delegates copied the look). On the same day he had selected Senator J. D. Vance to be his vice-presidential running mate. While he had a compelling personal life story and was manifestly very articulate, he had stood for public office only once and had not yet been in the US Senate for a full two years. He had also been openly very sceptical about Mr Trump when he ran in 2016. He was one of the first figures to pin the blame for the assassination event unambiguously on the Democrats. He was a risky pick.

It mattered not in the auditorium. He was a popular choice among conservative delegates. It looked like there was an heir to Mr Trump and Trumpism. The convention was a love fest. The acceptance speech by the nominee was not that memorable, but it was entirely adequate. Mr Trump had been politically resurrected. Mr Biden looked broken. Was it Mr Trump's election to lose?

CHAPTER FIVE

THE ROAD TO VICTORY

Exit the President. Enter the Vice President.
Electing the ex-President

The concept of the 'October Surprise' is well established in American presidential elections. It is the notion that some late-breaking and completely unexpected development or news has a decisive impact on the outcome. Most of the time the October Surprise cited has no such clout. This does not stop analysts – almost in the spirit of astrologists – waiting for it every four years.

In 2024, it was July, not October, which was the reservoir of surprises, and at least three of value. The first, as observed, was the length of the legal lifeline that the Supreme Court threw to Mr Trump on 1 July when it settled on the scope of presidential immunity in office. The second was how close the former President came to death on 13 July when a would-be assassin's bullet sailed an inch or two past his cranium. If he had been struck down then, especially as there was no Republican vice-presidential nominee even named at that moment, the Republican National Convention and the entire electoral process would have been sent into a sudden tailspin.

It would be hard to conceive of what could come next that might rival such a sensation. Yet on 21 July, at around the time that most Americans on the East Coast would be tucking into lunch, and from his home in Delaware where he was recuperating from COVID, President Biden created his own blockbuster moment, announcing courtesy of X (the successor to Twitter), first, that he no longer wished to be considered for the Democratic nomination and, second, that he was now making way for Vice President Kamala Harris to fly the flag as the Administration contender.

This should not have been the thunderbolt that it was. The President had been on the ropes for the better part of a month after a debate appearance which sparked a crisis of confidence in his cognitive faculties and his ability to defeat Mr Trump when it came to the November vote. At first it was only comparatively obscure congressional figures who were prepared to contend publicly that the President should contemplate falling on his sword. When Nancy Pelosi, the former Speaker of the House of Representatives, entered the discussion as to what Mr Biden should do with the strong steer that his time was up, then this was a more serious proposition.

The President had been adamant that he was not about to disappear and that he remained the best, indeed only, shot that the Democrats had of preventing Mr Trump returning to Washington. He had, after all, beaten him before. His poll ratings were not great, but it was still a close race. He had virtually all of the delegates to the coming Democratic National Convention in Chicago at his calling, and there was no means of forcing him out if he would not walk the plank. Even the nuclear option of invoking the XXVth Amendment of the Constitution would, hypothetically, suspend him as the serving President but technically it would not derail him as the Democratic nominee.

At some point either during the Republican Convention or shortly afterwards, Mr Biden had changed his mind. He offered his Vice President (and indeed his most senior aides) little notion of his great decision. Allowing for the late timing, it was arguably the most disorderly electoral abdication in recent American history (Lyndon Johnson's stunning exit from a candidacy took place in March 1968, which allowed his colleagues more time to think about what to do).

On the one hand, Mr Biden's abrupt shift was a gift to Kamala Harris as it soon became clear that she was the only person in a position to succeed him (particularly as he had backed her rather than, as he could have done, remained neutral or silent on who should come after him). On the other hand, she had been offered precious little time (107 days) to construct her own campaign.

Irrespective of these considerations, the spotlight which had been firmly on Mr Trump (to his considerable advantage and satisfaction) suddenly swung in the opposite direction. The political narrative was all about the Vice President. It was swiftly obvious that there would be a stampede towards her. While a few individuals mooted the notion that a contest or an event that could be branded a competition might be a sound move for everyone (including Ms Harris), the over-whelming urge was to get on with it. Virtually every major figure and sectional interest within the Democratic Party had endorsed the Vice President within 48 hours. The only prom-inent holdout was ex-President Obama (thought to harbour his own doubts about how Ms Harris would fare against Mr Trump and temperamentally disinclined to favour an anointment over a contested election) and his wife Michelle. They waited a full five days before backing the Vice President. By then, the Democratic National Committee (comprised mostly of Biden people) had adopted a new set of rules which would legitimise the transfer of authority occurring.

The response within the Democratic Party as a whole was shameless relief and the belief that the presidential contest could now be reset to their advantage. Praise was heaped upon Mr Biden not only for standing down but for his record in office. This had a strange look to it. If the Democratic establishment were to be regarded as the fountain of truth, then the President had achieved so much in less than four years that his face should be carved upon Mount Rushmore. This begged the question as to why, if he had been so capable, was he off to the knacker's yard. The sheer sugar rush of the situation was extraordinary. The demoralised Democratic base was rejuvenated. Millions of dollars from donors reluctant to embrace Mr Biden out of fear that this was money destined for the drain almost hurled their riches at the Vice President. The polls immediately tightened. There was the sense of an entirely new race that she could win.

It seemed as if the Republicans thought the same. Mr Trump struggled to settle upon a line of attack on his opponent. He started with the charge that she had been part of a great cover-up of exactly how steep Mr Biden's mental decline had become, but that did not trigger much interest. He referred to a coup d'etat (not the best line, in the light of what happened in January 2021). He used a live interview at the National Association of Black Journalists annual convention to question her racial identity, claiming that she once insisted she was Indian but now was black. This seemed distasteful and not many Republicans wanted to repeat that thesis. Having made the news (not always in a positive way) for weeks on end, she, not he, was the headline.

In retrospect, the first two weeks or so of August was as good as it could possibly get for the Vice President. She secured the nomination through an online roll call from 1 to 5 August. Her selection of Tim Walz, the Governor of Minnesota, who had a humble background, a folksy approach and revelled in having been a sports coach and teacher initially went down well. Only later would it become clear that parts of his life story involved fantasy and fabrication, leading he himself to admit in the single vice-presidential debate that he could be a 'knucklehead'.

Mr Walz was also the contender on the short-list for VP whom the progressive tendency in the Democratic Party found most appealing. The other three men thought to be in the frame, Governor Roy Cooper of North Carolina, Senator Mark Kelly of Arizona and Governor Josh Shapiro of Pennsylvania, were all of a more centrist hue and came from states which would be crucial to any electoral college majority being assembled by the Democratic candidate. Such was the surge in confidence that the replacement of the President by the Vice President had created that such tactical considerations were just disregarded. The Democratic Convention in Chicago was as much of a collective swoon as the Republican one had been a month before. The distinction was that many Democrats did not know that much about their new leader.

The Trump team continued to tie itself in knots about how to counter Ms Harris and blasted off in all directions. It was also clear from her astonishing fundraising receipts that it was likely to be outspent massively on TV advertising. The closest that the ex-President came to a political break during August was when Robert Kennedy Jr jettisoned his quixotic independent candidacy and threw in his lot with Mr Trump. The number of voters he could corral with him was, alas for Mr Trump, probably rather small. The disposal of Mr Biden made it easier for a few noted 'Never Trump' Republicans such as former congresswoman Liz Cheney and her father ex-Vice President Dick Cheney to back Ms Harris. She was a blank canvass who allowed voters to paint on whatever colours they chose.

She also had a reputation as a high-quality debater. After Mr Biden had detonated himself in the Atlanta showdown back in June, Mr Trump had been vigorously demanding many more debates before election day. Once Ms Harris was his opponent he changed his tune. It appeared as if he might duck out of the second agreed debate which was to be on 10 September in Philadelphia with the ABC network acting as the host. No remotely plausible alibi could be mustered for such a withdrawal. He went ahead and, while nowhere near as poor as Mr Biden had been about 11 weeks previously, he was playing second fiddle to the Vice President, who was far more confident with the format and trained her fire upon him. An election that seemed set to be a referendum on Mr Biden's age risked being recast as one where the American public were asked to be part of a plebiscite on the virtues of Mr Trump instead.

Deadlock followed (or so it appeared on the basis of the opinion polls). The Vice President was usually ahead in the popular vote but with an edge that was closer to that of Mrs Clinton in 2016 than Mr Biden four years later. This was always a matter of concern for Democratic strategists. The seven swing states (Arizona, Georgia, Michigan, Nevada, North Carolina, Pennsylvania and Wisconsin) were so close that not one of them could even be deemed to be leaning towards one candidate or the other. Ms Harris obtained some coverage from celebrity supporters (with Taylor Swift endorsing her straight after her 10 September debate showing). Mr Trump might have got a very small bump from the vice-presidential debate on October 1st where Senator Vance was considerably smoother and more at ease than Governor Walz. Would that count for anything?

October not only declined to produce its supposed 'surprise'; it felt like one long slog towards the finishing line. Millions upon millions of dollars were raised and spent in the seven states that mattered while the rest of the country was entitled to feel that it was being thoroughly ignored.

The content and tone of the contest was harsh and heated. Strange 'issues' such as whether feral illegal migrants were really stealing and eating domestic pets in an area of Ohio made the news, while a host of somewhat more important matters (the economy and foreign policy) were marginalised. The indications in the states that had the most charitable early voting laws was that, despite the dismal spectacle in front of them, this would be a high turnout election (although lower in the end than 2020, which had been very high by American levels). The Democrats took heart from this, although there was data to indicate that the Republicans who had dissuaded their supporters from voting by mail in 2020 had learnt their lesson.

The campaigns settled into a pattern that reflected the personalities of the contenders. The Democratic rallies were upbeat, and the Vice President was punchy even though she did not delve much into the details of policies. The chant instead was that 'we are not going back.' Her biggest challenge was how to convince undecided voters that she would be a different President from Mr Biden (whose approval ratings rarely rose above 40% and who had disappeared from national sight) while not repudiating an administration in which she was the Vice President. It was a conundrum that she never quite resolved. She was the Not Trump (and Not Biden) contender more than anything else. She had to hope that would be enough to see her home.

Mr Trump did have broad themes, normally the cost-of-living crisis, border security and the need for 'mass deportation' and a firm commitment to avoid being entangled in foreign wars. As he had a lead on all these spheres in the opinion polls it made sense for him to focus here. His campaign rallies did not stick to the script with sufficient rigour. He meandered too easily. An example of this, and it was to borrow from Governor Walz's favourite word 'weird', was a strange digression in which he appeared to opine on what might be politely described as the size of the late Arnold Palmer's golf bag. Almost anything could emerge when he opened his mouth.

On balance, and it was not an enchanting spectacle, Mr Trump was making the news more often than his opponent managed. His long and varied career in the media spotlight was an asset. He had a better sense of how to attract attention than his rival did. He took on potentially challenging interviews with podcasters who his target demographics were known to favour. His best public relations moment was on October 21 when he put in a shift at McDonald's and did not seem incredible in the uniform or shaking fries. His least effective event would be a major rally at Madison Square Garden, New York City, when a conservative comedian, Tony Hinchcliffe, called Puerto Rico 'a floating island of garbage'. As the Hispanic vote was becoming central to Mr Trump this was not the most useful of comments. Distancing himself from them, let alone simply denouncing them, was not done well. Fortunately, and not for the first time, President Biden accidently came to Mr Trump's rescue by insinuating that Mr Trump's supporters were the real 'garbage', and then denying that he said it.

A very long campaign for one candidate (Mr Trump) and a far, far shorter one for the other (Ms Harris) eventually came to its close. On the morning of the election – Tuesday 5 November – the phrase 'too close to call' still retained its currency. The consensus position was that it was very probable that the Vice President would, as Mrs Clinton and Mr Biden had done before her, carry the popular vote but by a small margin, while if pushed really forcefully the alleged experts would predict that it was more likely than not that Mr Trump would squeak by in the electoral college, but that it would all come down to a handful of ballot papers probably in Pennsylvania. A clean result on the night seemed challenging. A few days might pass (as in 2020) before any of the networks could identify a winner with enough confidence. The threat of lawsuits was real. As far as Congress was concerned, there was a settled agreement among those who follow the Senate that the Republicans were well placed to restore a majority there by only a slender 51–49 margin with West Virginia and Montana moving to the GOP. The House of Representatives was much harder to read, but it would not be a shock if the Democrats gained enough seats to win there. Whoever took the White House was therefore condemned to divided government.

It was not how it worked out. The overall result was more conclusive. It became apparent from early in the night that Mr Trump was in better shape than he had been in 2020 and in a number of early states, even though he would be defeated, he was obtaining more votes than in 2016 as well (New Jersey was a prime example of this). Florida, which had been very closely fought in 2016 and 2020 with Mr Trump narrowly taking its electoral college votes both times, was a blowout for him. Texas, when the polls shut there, was a similar story. Ohio would be a walk in the park.

The swing states would swing as of one towards him. The Trump lead was tight but was not tiny. He would win Arizona by 5.5 points, Georgia by 2.2 points, Michigan by 1.4 points, Nevada (which he had lost in 2016 and 2020) by 3.1 points, North Carolina (which had been with Trump in 2016 and 2020) by 3.3 points, Pennsylvania by 1.7 points and Wisconsin by 0.9 points. His electoral college outcome was hence virtually identical to 2016, except that he added Nevada.

What really shook the commentators was that unlike 2016

he also prevailed in the popular vote. Although his tally would narrow as overseas ballots were counted, he had taken almost exactly a majority of all the votes cast (and certainly would if spoilt and void ballots are to be disregarded). Even his admirers had not seen that one coming. This led to some rather odd claims from certain Republicans that Mr Trump had conjured up a 'landslide'. This was not borne out by the numbers. His popular vote win (1.5%) was smaller than the one by which Mrs Clinton had beaten him eight years earlier and clearly less than that which George W. Bush managed to hold in 2004 when he had defeated Senator John Kerry (although his electoral college total was smaller than Mr Trump enjoyed in both 2016 and 2024). It had been a close race and the states that had been expected to be the most marginal did indeed live up to that billing. Yet, it was not extremely close. Mr Trump was not far off coming in first in both Minnesota and New Hampshire.

It was a similar tale of Republican strength being underestimated in Congress. The Senate fell to them by 53–47 rather than 51–49 courtesy of snatching Ohio and Pennsylvania (although the sitting Democratic Senator, Bob Casey, was reluctant to concede) as well as in West Virginia and Montana. The Democrats almost lost in Michigan, Nevada and Wisconsin as well and were miles away from victory in Florida and Texas, which had been touted as their best opportunities. The nearest the Republicans came to a loss was in Nebraska against an independent rather than a Democrat. The House was genuinely competitive, but the Republicans hung on there.

Electoral politics is about expectations as well as numbers. The Republicans had beaten expectations. Mr Trump had won the popular vote when few thought that he would do so. He had triumphed in every single one of the swing states, stronger as might have been expected in the southern sector (Arizona, Georgia, Nevada and North Carolina) than in the 'blue wall' of the Mid West (Michigan, Pennsylvania and Wisconsin). Most observers thought the Vice President would come first in at least one of those three battlegrounds. She had outspent him there. The Republicans were in complete control of the Senate. The House was tight but in their hands.

The sense of a mandate for Mr Trump was therefore more pronounced than he could have hoped. This time round, having brought the Senate with him, he would be, to revisit the formula set out in Chapter Three, that rare item, a Category A President, a standing that afforded him a mandate.

Who voted for whom? The exit polls are instructive. There had been much talk before the day itself that the 2024 election would produce the largest gender gap in US electoral history. It did not. Mr Trump won men by 13 points. Ms Harris took women by eight points. That 21-point differential is lower than in 2020 when it was 23 points and 2016 when it was a point higher. It was Mr Trump's best performance of the three contests among men to be sure, but it was also his most superior outcome among women of his three presidential outings as well. There is not much data here to support the charge that misogyny ruled the roost. Gender was not critical.

It was claimed that the Trump camp were masterminding an under-the-radar mass conversion of black voters, with men again the most likely to switch towards him. The statistics refute this too. There was a degree of movement to the ex-President, but it was modest. In 2016 the edge to the Democrats among black men was 69 points. In 2020 it was 60 points. In 2024 it was 56 points. Black women were staunchly loyal to the Democrats even if their margin slipped slightly from a whopping 90 points in 2016 for Mrs Clinton to 81 points in 2020 for Mr Biden and 84 points now. The Republicans might once have been the Party of Lincoln to black citizens. They are not today.

There was more behind the assertion that Mr Trump had made himself attractive to younger voters. Mr Trump had lost those aged 18–29 by 19 points in 2016 and 24 points in 2020 but dragged his deficit back to 11 points in 2024. This was useful but would not explain any swing state.

Who then were the new Trump voters, and might they have been seminal in swing states?

In one section of Americans, it was not so much about being 'new' as returning to the fold. Voters in rural areas had embraced Mr Trump by 27 points in 2016 (a gigantic swing to him compared with Mr Romney four years previously) but this fell back sharply in 2020 to 15 points. Normal service would be restored in 2024 with a 30-point lead which did move the needle.

The standout racial demographic was not the white vote (basically static compared with 2020) or as described above the black electorate (a small shift to Mr Trump) but the Latino citizens. In 2016 Latino men had preferred Mrs Clinton to Mr Trump by a thumping 31 points. That figure came down in 2020 as Mr Biden vanquished Mr Trump by a lesser but hardy 23 points. In 2024, the Republican candidate won this group of voters by 12 points. Latino women stuck with the Democrats but even here their edge halved between 2016 and 2024 (from 44 to 22 points). This is the sub-result which should be the cause of the most soul-searching for the Democrats.

The most significant issue by far, and the best explanation for the result, was the economy. If an elector thought that the economy was in excellent condition, then they split for Ms Harris by an enormous 89%–10% margin (but only 5% held that outlook). If they judged the economy to be good rather than excellent, they favoured Ms Harris by an even more imposing 91%–8% (27% of those who cast ballots contended the economy was in good order). If they asserted that the economy was 'not so good' then they broke for Mr Trump by 54%–44% (35% of voters were in this cohort) and if they condemned the economy as poor, he won by 87% to 10% (and a full third of the electorate were in this category). Put another way, when asked which contender they had most trust in on the economy, Mr Trump was the choice by 52% to 46% and the economy was, as it had been throughout the campaign, the single most important issue identified by electors.

The Trump restoration was realised by reconnecting with rural voters whom he had lost in 2020, a really intriguing sharp shift in his favour among those of Hispanic descent and appearing to be the figure most likely to fix an economy that had been beset by high inflation and interest rates.

If Mr Trump and the Republicans are now to retain the affections of the coalition that they have assembled, then stimulating the economy with their promised tax cuts and other measures will be by far the most pressing matter to face the President, the Senate and the House leadership in 2025.

CHAPTER SIX

TRUMP AT HOME

Substantial cuts in taxation will be the centre-piece of his domestic agenda

What will President Trump II do with his victory? The party 'platform', comprising individual 'planks', is the closest that the US political system comes to a UK-style manifesto. It is adopted at the national convention every four years. It is not in any way binding on a presidential candidate or those seeking office in the House of Representatives and Senate and there is no 'doctrine of mandate' associated with it. The platform is best seen as an expression of identity, a statement of intent or a line of travel, but it does show what the GOP leaders are thinking.

The 2024 Republican Platform adopted in July 2024 is, in these terms, striking. It is short, strident and in tune with Donald Trump in content and style. It is more akin to an extended tweet than a formal document. It has its own position on the English language, with Capital Letters in the Middle of Sentences for No Obvious Reason, some block capitals for emphasis (such as DRILL, BABY, DRILL, summarising the 'Unleash American Energy' ambition) and considerable enthusiasm for exclamation marks!!!

It is very different to the 2016 platform which was an uneasy (and rather lengthy) compromise draft between traditional Republican doctrine and the preferences of the insurgent nominee. In 2020, a normal convention was rendered impossible by COVID-19 and the platform referred back to 2016. This is hence the first pure and unadulterated articulation of the President Trump Republican Party. It contains aspects of pragmatism (notably on abortion) but plenty of elements of radicalism as well.

There are key domestic policy aspirations which would have significant impact beyond the US too.

The first chapter, entitled 'Defeat Inflation and quickly bring down all prices' indicates a priority but not much in terms of precise measures. It places its weight on 'terminating the Socialist Green New Deal' (a signature piece of legislation enacted by the Democrats) along with pledges to 'cut federal spending and burdensome regulations'. Social Security and Medicare are exempt from that drive. It is reasonable to conclude that, despite the rhetoric, the federal government will not be shrunk fast.

The second chapter, headlined 'Seal the border, and stop the migrant invasion', is a core mission. It would involve completing the barrier or 'wall' that made modest progress in the initial Trump term, aggressively seeking the deportation of 'millions of illegal migrants' and enhancing border security overall by 'moving thousands of Troops currently stationed overseas to our own Southern Border.' With Mr Trump elected, this was now actually likely to happen which will make life very uncomfortable indeed for those countries where those to be deported originally came from and for those nations which will lose American soldiers from within their boundaries as they are withdrawn to patrol the US itself.

The third chapter, namely 'Build the greatest economy in history,' contains the measures that, along with the border and immigration, are of the most importance once the Trump presidency is restored.

The Tax Cuts and Jobs Act 2017, probably the most

significant legislative act of the first Trump term, cut corporate taxes (as a whole) on a permanent basis, but the reductions in taxation for individuals through doubling the standard deduction and expanding the Child Tax Credit included a vital sunset clause. The Republicans want to make these provisions entrenched as well. Furthermore, '… we will eliminate Taxes on Tips for millions of Restaurant and Hospitality workers and pursue additional Tax Cuts!' All of which might well, as is asserted in the platform, 'spur economic growth for all Americans' but would also be expensive. There may be tension between slashing taxes and eliminating inflation.

There are other provisions in the economy section that are intriguing in their novelty. The platform takes a strongly sympathetic line towards cryptocurrencies and opposes government efforts to put limits on them. It backs incentives for investing in AI. It is keen on the economic utility of outer space. A cynical soul would note that some prominent billionaire backers of Mr Trump have made their cash out of cryptocurrency and Elon Musk's endorsement and cash were extremely valuable commodities, but this could be a coincidence. In any case, a more permissive US approach in these sectors is bound to have some knock-on effects.

The final series of initiatives which will matter outside of the United States relate to energy supplies and climate change. The slogan DRILL, BABY, DRILL is not for show. It would plainly be a major goal for a new Trump Administration to obtain added energy self-sufficiency by allowing for a massive increase in extraction with far less deference towards environmental objections than exists today. It is also absolutely evident that the Trump White House would treat the whole climate change agenda with an undisguised disdain encapsulated by the cast-iron commitment to enforce the 'cancelling of Biden's Electric Vehicles and other Mandates and preventing the importation of Chinese vehicles'.

How much of what the Republican Platform envisions actually occurs depends on the attitude of Congress and whether the party can hold its discipline in the House of Representatives (where it has a super-slender majority) and maintain unity in the Senate (which it is likely to do although there will be tensions over how large the deficit should be). This is an approach that should certainly be taken seriously by business. As what happens to the US economy has immense implications elsewhere, it will affect the whole world.

The federal government budget under a new Trump Administration is thus of central importance. In order to anticipate and assess what the Trump Effect (especially on the tax side of the ledger) might be, the rational starting point is where the US economy stood in 2024, what sort of shape it was in both in regard to the public finances and certain fundamentals such as growth, inflation and jobs and what the best estimate is of what would occur across the whole budgetary and economic horizon if existing policy were simply left in place with minimal amendment. This would provide us with a valuable baseline.

One of the many purposes of the Congressional Budget Office (CBO), established under a major piece of law in 1974, is to do exactly what has just been set out: the full overview of the American landscape. The most recent such comprehensive analysis, and the last one to be released before the presidential election, was its *An Update to the Budget and Economic Outlook 2024 to 2034*. As a studiously non-partisan institution, with some similarity in this regard to the much younger Office for Budget Responsibility in the United Kingdom, its findings have a near gold standard quality to them.

This document soberly sets out what should happen in fiscal terms 'if laws governing taxes and spending generally remain unchanged.'

The CBO anticipated that for Fiscal Year 2024 (which started on 1 October 2023), federal revenues (overwhelmingly derived from taxation) would be $4.9 trillion and the outlays (mostly expenditure) would be $6.8 trillion. That creates a federal budget deficit for the year of $1.9 trillion (a tidy sum), an advance on Fiscal Year 2023, which technically should be thought of as $2.0 trillion (due to a quirk in the calendar, in 2023 1 October fell on a Sunday so certain government payments were made on the preceding Friday which caused the Fiscal Year 2023 deficit to be artificially slightly higher and the Fiscal Year 2024 deficit artificially slightly lower than had 1 October 2023 been a weekday).

The deficit would therefore be a sizeable 7% of GDP in 2024 but was set to be reduced to 6.5% in the year afterwards. From 2027 if current policy continued (which would mean that such tax revenue lost under the Tax Cuts and Jobs Act 2017 would be regained in 2026 as the sunset clause made its mark), the deficit would decrease further. In the longer term, rising social spending related to a population that was collectively ageing would push it upwards again so that it nudged 7% once more (as in 2024), a level which the CBO noted was 'significantly more than the 3.7% that deficits have averaged over the past 50 years'. This in turn would have negative connotations for the debt to Gross Domestic Product statistics. In 2024 this stood at 99% (almost exactly the same as the UK) but would move up to 122% by 2034 ('surpassing its previous high of 106%'). With revenues (assuming continued policy) broadly flat from 2024 to 2034 and spending edging upward, a 7% of GDP deficit would become normal.

It is worth explaining what federal government spending

involves and why controlling it is challenging.

In Fiscal Year 2024, outlays were 24.2% of US GDP (revenues, by contrast, were 17.2% of US GDP).

Of that sum, there is a three-way division. Mandatory spending (where a change in the law would be needed to reduce it) was 14.7% of GDP, discretionary spending (which can be altered annually by Capitol Hill) was 6.3% of GDP and net interest payments (which could be cut only by a US default) were 3.1%. Within that mandatory section social security (pensions in UK terminology) was 5.1%, the major healthcare programmes of Medicaid (a joint federal–state scheme for those on low incomes) and Medicare (an exclusively federal health insurance package for those aged 65 and older) was 5.8% and other mandatory expenditure (much of which involves military veterans) swallowed 3.8%. This is close to politically untouchable. Mr Trump shied away from reform before and that is still his stance.

Which, as net interest repayments cannot realistically be cut on a whim either, leaves discretionary spending. This is in turn split between defence spending at 3.0% in 2024 (or $849 billion in cash terms, the highest in the world by an enormous margin) and non-defence spending at 3.3% (or $948 billion as a cash sum). It should now be manifest that the task of slashing what is a historically very high federal deficit (particularly as recession is not the catalyst for it) by spending cuts is very limited.

Over the ten-year period 2024–2034 what confronts American politicians becomes yet more stark. Assuming no policy adjustment whatsoever by the close of this period net interest repayments will grow to hit 4.1% and to account for about one-sixth of all federal spending. That is a lot of red ink. Cumulative federal revenues looking ahead are estimated at $62.814 trillion, outlays at $84.897 trillion and deficits at \$22.083 trillion. It is difficult to see how this could be comfortably sustained.

The CBO also has short-term and medium-term projections for the main economic indicators. It is not roaringly optimistic about economic growth. This was a sprightly 3.3% in 2023 (to the utter amazement of many professional economists who thought growth would be negative that year) but rowed back to 2.0% in 2024 (putting nails in the political coffin of the Democratic Party). Looking ahead, 'In CBO projections, economic growth remains steady at 2.0% in 2025 before settling at roughly 1.8% in 2026 and later years. A surge in immigration that began in 2021 [and condemned the Biden Administration in the eyes of many electors] continues through 2026 [not if Mr Trump can help it] expanding the labour force and boosting economic output.' When that ends, growth will flatline. The ball-and-chain restricting economic expansion is, once again, a consistently ageing population.

Other CBO predictions include inflation which, again assuming no policy re-evaluation, would fall from 2.7% in 2024 (well down on 2023) to roughly 2.0% by 2026 and be stable from then onwards. Interest rates, which have started to come down in the US, would (again only with a policy status quo), carry on that path until the end of 2026 but after that be more likely to increase than to fall. The unemployment rate which in 2024 was only 3.9% would stay close to that figure until 2030. Average wage increases, which in 2024 were 4.0%, would slow over time to 2.7%. The United States would, bar a sharp policy shift, continue to run large trade deficits throughout these ten years.

It is fair to say there is not much in these numbers which Mr Trump and his allies will be cheering. They are firmly of the view that growth needs to be rejuvenated and that will demand new policies. Reducing taxation – as the Republican

Party Platform articulated – would be the main device here.

The tax measures that Mr Trump would pledge to seek while on the stump are many and varied.

His absolutely first priority is to render permanent all of the individual and estate tax cuts in the Tax Cuts and Jobs Act 2017, which unless the law is updated would be temporary and so expire by 2026. These include, among other items, an increase in the standard deduction (the total that persons can earn before income tax kicks in), lower marginal income tax rates for most income brackets and an increase to the estate tax (or inheritance tax in British vocabulary) exemption. If this were to be the only output of the next Trump Administration (which would be a disappointment to it of some order) then the CBO estimates (others disagree somewhat) it would slash revenue by $4.6 trillion by 2034.

This is far from the only objective for the President. He would like to extend the 2017 Act further.

He would do so by abolishing the current cap on SALT (State and Local Taxes) tax deductions that Americans can claim, but under the 2017 Act by no more than $10,000. This is of most potency in states with high taxation within their own borders. The very existence of the cap led a set of GOP members of the House of Representatives from California and New York to vote against the Act.

Mr Trump would also prefer to revisit his original preference in 2017 to cut corporation tax all the way down to 15% (very low or, in his mind, internationally competitive) and not the 21% enacted.

The incoming President has also called for the Act to be amended to restore the capacity of US companies immediately to deduct the cost of investment in equipment from tax.

The above might be regarded as eradicating necessary but unappealing compromises made in his first term to ensure that a tax package was agreed by Congress at all in favour of a purer policy.

The Trump blueprint would not stop there. While campaigning in 2024 he suggested a completely new set of tax reductions that he would want Congress to entrench into additional new legislation.

The list here is long and intriguing (and it has the strong element of electoral inducements to it).

Mr Trump wants to end income tax on the tips which hospitality industry workers often rely on. This was an enticing suggestion to Latino employees more than most and went down well in the state of Nevada where hotels, casinos and restaurants are an atypically large section of the local economy. The proposal was so popular in that silver state that Ms Harris and the Democrats had to match it.

He also promoted allowing citizens to deduct from their taxes the costs involved in automobile loan interest expenditure, much as they have for many decades been able to do for mortgage interest. This probably went down well everywhere but was designed to attract support in Michigan, a state where automobile production remains a substantial section of the economy (his vocal attacks on electric cars imported from China will have been well received in the Detroit area of the same state too).

He advocated eliminating income tax on social security benefits (about half of Americans are rich enough to pay some). This was soothing to a demographic in which his support was not reliable.

He cheered the notion of disposing of income tax (and possibly payroll tax which funds the social security system, but this was never quite certain) on all overtime earnings. A pitch to the workers.

More ambiguously and perhaps better seen as an ambition

rather than anything stronger, he was enticed by the idea of a bespoke income tax arrangement for police officers, firefighters, veterans, active-duty members of the military and others considered to be 'first responders' to the public.

The candidate also expressed some empathy for a tax credit that can be claimed by family carers. Senator J. D. Vance also trumpeted an increase in the child tax credit to $5,000 per juvenile but Mr Trump never explicitly agreed with him on that (partly because he was rarely asked his opinion). There may have been other tax reduction kites floated at the many rallies Mr Trump addressed.

This is a formidable prospectus. How much might it cost in lost revenue? How could it be paid for?

These are not straightforward questions to address. The most detailed attempt to do so is arguably that of the Tax Foundation. This is a think tank that has been in business for a decent stretch of time (since 1937) and which while on the centre-right is a mainstream conservative organisation fiscally in that while it regards taxation as an impediment to the economy it is resolutely in favour of lower federal budget deficits, does not overclaim the growth benefits of tax cuts and is for free trade not tariffs. It is, in this author's assessment, a better body to rely on for arithmetical authenticity than those on the other side of the philosophical fence, whose dislike of Mr Trump may taint their judgement here.

The Tax Foundation had (by October 2024) crunched the numbers about as hard as anyone could do.

Their topline preliminary estimate was that the net loss of tax revenues over ten years would be of the order of $3 trillion. Long-run growth would increase by 0.8% per annum (a big rise), long-run wages by the same figure, the capital stock by 1.7% and total employment by about 600,000 jobs (not such a striking conclusion allowing for the size of the US labour market). As will be revealed below, these headline findings allow for a considerable array of conditional calculations and caveats.

The Foundation started with what Mr Trump would regard as the bare minimum, making permanent those aspects of the Tax Cuts and Jobs Act 2017 and nothing else. This would reduce revenues by $3.4 trillion if the existing SALT cap limit were not to be abolished. If it were scrapped this would add $1 trillion to that assessment. If the estate tax cut were also to be a permanent feature this would add another $205 billion and the business tax deduction for research and development and other features the President deems essential will put on $643 billion. The total loss comes to $5.3 trillion.

The five major additional tax cuts championed by Mr Trump – exempting tips from income tax, and the same for social security benefits, introducing a deduction for car loan interest payments, a cut in corporation tax to 15% and removing overtime from the reaches of income tax – could together cost a further $2.5 trillion, taking the combined taxation revenue lost to $7.8 trillion (or about 12.5% of the cumulative tax take for 2024–2034 that the CBO asserted would come in to the federal coffers).

Some money would flow back to the US Treasury. Mr Trump has urged that the green tax credits devised by the Inflation Reduction Act of 2022 passed at the behest of the Biden Administration should be done away with (and few Republicans will disagree with him). That will save $921 billion. If a 20% across-the-board tariff on imports (plus a higher penalty on China) is embraced, then this could be something of a money-spinner, securing $3.8 trillion over ten years. It is a possibility that the Tax Foundation itself detests, insisting that it would offset more than two-thirds of the long-run economic benefits of his tax reductions. The maths then becomes $7.8

trillion minus $4.8 trillion and therefore the net $3 trillion in tax revenue forgone cited earlier, a much smaller overall revenue sacrifice. That tally is one framed by what is called 'conventional accounting'. If 'dynamic accounting' is allowed for (which incorporates positive behavioural adjustment in the light of tax incentives) then the revenue that disappears is a little over $2.5 trillion over the decade. Mr Trump would back this.

That could still, the Tax Foundation surmises, be a rosy analysis. As the pledge to permit the arrival of a caregivers' allowance does not appear to be a firm promise, it has not been scored in the figures. In a similar spirit, the expansion of the child tax credit associated with J. D. Vance but not as yet hailed by the President himself has been completely excluded too (which may be a blessing as it involves a chunky $2.432 trillion in taxation proceeds). If one were to count them in, then the revised findings for the overall tax impact would essentially double from just over $3 trillion to a tiny part below $6 trillion (with dynamic accounting considerations reducing both sums by around one-sixth of those levels).

This is not an exercise in imaginary economics. With the Republicans in command of all three branches of the federal government only until the 2026 mid-term elections, when their oversight of Washington politics could be interrupted (past form firmly suggests that they will lose the House), then they need to move hard and fast. It is not a surreal wager to presume that the temporary provisions of the Tax Cuts and Jobs Act 2017 will be set in stone and other Trump tax cuts enacted.

What will all this mean (a) for the American economy and (b) for the international economy at large?

A tax cut on this scale would surely be expected to be a stimulus for economic growth, and that is why the stock market whooped once the election outcome had registered. This may be a boon for the person selected as the Republican presidential nominee in 2028, but a lot of water has to flow under the overall political bridge before that hour is upon us. It is also fair to anticipate that more vigorous economic growth will have an offsetting effect on the loss of tax revenues. It is also reasonable to look at the sums and think that, with revenues lower and the forces behind mandatory expenditure still to be contended with, the federal deficit and national debt will be higher (unless the new Department for Government Efficiency to be steered by Mr Musk and Mr Ramaswamy can produce the sort of astronomical $2 trillion in savings in non-defence discretionary spending that is mooted). There is, to repeat, little out there which suggests the mandatory spending programmes will be restricted.

Growth is to be applauded. It may be accompanied by inflationary signals and a higher debt burden.

Which is certainly how the Federal Reserve is likely to see the situation. One of the main factors in why US interest rates have remained at comparatively high levels, and started to be reduced only from September 2024, is that the Fed regards a significant component of recent US inflation as the side-effect of a fiscal policy that lacks discipline (on the expenditure side) with a rampant federal deficit.

The Federal Open Market Committee which sets interest rates may well come to the view that this, from its standpoint, undesirable state of affairs will continue under the second Trump White House but with lower tax revenues, rather than excess non-defence discretionary spending, the source of mischief. The Fed also regards immigration as a benign economic element in life and will be perturbed that cutting it off will make the US labour market tighter and put wages on a higher trajectory than they would have been without Mr Trump returning to the Oval Office. All told, Trumponomics II could involve stronger growth in the short-term (and beyond if the Tax Foundation is correct) but with US interest rates remaining higher than they might otherwise have been (and which the CBO allows for in its projections), and the dollar consistently higher (influencing global oil prices outside of the US) than in a different context. These features will have a tangible impact on the international economy.

CHAPTER SEVEN

AMERICA FIRST: THE TERMS OF TRADE

*A far more assertive stance on tariffs will be
the theme of US international economic policy*

'For decades, our politicians sold our jobs and livelihoods to the highest bidder overseas with unfair trade deals and a blind faith in the siren song of globalism.'

The above quotation is not from George Galloway's Workers Party manifesto in the UK general election of 2024 (although it could have been) but it appears in the preamble to the Republican Party Platform, a document titled *America First: A Return to Common Sense*. It is inconceivable that such a statement would have emerged when George W. Bush, John McCain or Mitt Romney were the nominees of the GOP, let alone Ronald Reagan, George H. W. Bush or Robert Dole. It would have been an excessive choice of words for all recent Democratic nominees as well. It is stronger language than that articulated when Donald Trump was first the candidate in 2016. Its inclusion should not be disregarded as accidental or simple rhetoric. It is telling us something.

American trade policy and hence its approach to international economics more broadly will be very different. This will be a major extension, a real step change, in a shift that has been coming.

On the campaign stump, Mr Trump frequently referred to unfair trade and his determination to deal with it by assertive measures of his own. At one stage, he referred to 'tariffs' as 'the most beautiful word in the dictionary'. If so, he may be interested to know that it has its origins in the Arabic *arafa* (meaning to notify) and a Persian term for 'an inventory of fees to be paid'. This fused into the Ottoman Turkish 'ta'rife' ('a list of prices or table of customs rates'). Over time it entered European (and then American) discourse via the Italian *tariffa* and finally to the French term *tariff*. For most mainstream economists (and many in the business community who conduct trade across borders), wherever the word comes from, it is close to a profanity in their opinion and has been for more than 75 years now. Under America First, it is firmly back in the frame.

What should lead an observer to believe this is not bluster but the birth of a sizeable initiative, one that whether it proves to be effective in its objectives or not, will alter the entire dialogue of economic conversations between Washington and its erstwhile allies and force others to think deeply about how they respond to it, and whether they too dilute their devotion to free trade?

The first element to be conceded here is tariffs are hardly a novelty in US economic thinking. They have a very long history to them indeed. The second law to be passed by the newly created US Congress, signed into law on 4 July 1789, was the Tariff Act (the first legislation to be adopted was 'An Act to regulate the Time and Manner of administering certain Oaths' on 1 June, so it could be concluded that the Tariff Act was the first law of serious weight to be alighted on). It was the brainchild of Alexander Hamilton, the first Secretary of the Treasury (whose face has been on $10 bills since 1928) who was a pioneer of what would come to be called the 'infant industry' argument in favour of protectionism.

Furthermore, the founding President would have had

very little compunction in putting his name to it. The vast majority of US Presidents from 1789 to 1933 were vigorous protectionists. This includes all four of those whose images would be carved into Mount Rushmore as recognition of their contribution to the Republic: namely George Washington, Thomas Jefferson, Abraham Lincoln and Theodore Roosevelt.

Nor were they half-hearted on the subject.

In his 1790 State of the Union Address (then a written statement), Washington (who had stated proudly that he consumed no food 'but such as is made in America') insisted that a 'free people' would have to 'promote such manufactories as tend to render them independent of others for essential, particularly military, supplies.'

Thomas Jefferson had started as a comparative sceptic about tariffs, but once President said:

'… experience has taught me that manufactures are now as necessary to our independence as to our comfort: and if those who quote me as of a different opinion will keep pace with me in purchasing nothing foreign where an equivalent of domestic fabric can be obtained, without regard to price…'

Abraham Lincoln had extolled as early as 1847, 'Give us a protective tariff, and we shall have the greatest nation on earth' (the Make America Great Again line has been around for a while). During the Civil War (where tariffs were a seminal dispute between the North and the South), he sought to obtain a 44% tariff rate on all imports entering his section of the United States.

Theodore Roosevelt was no less unequivocal:

'The country has acquiesced in the wisdom of the protective-tariff principle. It is exceedingly undesirable that this system should be destroyed or that there should be violent and radical changes therein. Our past experience shows

that great prosperity in this country has always come under
a protective tariff.'

Even in the several decades after the Tariff Act of 1930 (or
'Smoot-Hawley' as it was dubbed after its congressional spon-
sors), Republican Presidents were willing to reach for tariffs as
a last resort and some of their most senior advisers retained a
nostalgic affection for protectionism. In 1971, Richard Nixon
exploited provisions of the by then archaic Trading with the
Enemy Act of 1917 to slap on a 10% import tariff as a reaction
to a balance of payments crisis that he faced. Alfred Eckles
Jr, the Chairman of the US International Trade Commission
under Ronald Reagan, would reminisce that between 1871
and 1913 'the average US tariff in dutiable imports never fell
below 38% and GDP grew 4.3% annually, twice the pace
of free trade Britain and well above the US average of the
twentieth century' (it should be remembered that until 1913
there was no constitutional consent for a federal income tax,
so tariffs often generated 95% of tax takings). Even George
W. Bush found himself, reluctantly, reaching for high steel
tariffs in a 2002 crisis.

It is, therefore, very hard to articulate that tariffs are
somehow 'unAmerican' and that if Mr Trump embraces them
as completely as it appears he may, that he has no history he
can cite in his favour. Like much of Trumpism, his position
is not a deviation but a reversion. What academic economists
and a multitude of CEOs might think is immaterial to him
here.

The second factor to be acknowledged is that the law already
allows the President huge scope to introduce new tariffs with
few constraints on that activism if it is adopted. It is emphatically not the case that Mr Trump would need new legislative
authority to implement his agenda (but he would happily

sign into law any such supplementary authority if Congress offered it to him). Although the Constitution itself is plain that Congress is in the driving seat in this theatre as 'The Congress shall have the power to lay and collect taxes, Duties … To regulate commerce with foreign nations' (Article I, Section VIII), it has been willing to delegate this capacity to the Executive for many decades and the Supreme Court has ruled that it has the ability to do so as long as it could reclaim its formal authority at any point by legislation should it wish to do so.

The oldest such weapon that can still be used is the afore-mentioned Tariff Act of 1930 (or Smoot-Hawley). It was not repealed from the statute book. Section 338 of this legislation allows the President to impose additional tariffs [additional because some tariffs would be customary] of up to 50% on any country that discriminates against US products, and it allows the President to block imports completely for any country that discriminates against US products. This is a power which has not been deployed for more than 70 years, but it could come out of retirement.

There are three other landmark laws which are more likely to be cited by the new Administration.

The Trade Expansion Act of 1962, signed into law by John F. Kennedy. Section 232 affords the President broad powers to adjust imports into the United States if they are found to be a threat to US national security, including through the imposition of tariffs if that was decided necessary. It was widely held that Mr Nixon in 1971 could have gone down this route as an alternative to the one that he took (rather controversially) when he was faced with an intense economic storm. At a (very) long stretch, this wording could be taken as allowing all imports to be deemed a threat to the US.

These measures may be triggered either by the Department

of Commerce doing so of its own volition or at the direction of the Oval Office. The Department would have up to 270 days to study and to make a determination, there would follow up to 90 days for the President to agree or not with that conclusion and up to 15 days after that to take action. In reality, this could be much faster.

The Trade Act of 1974 is an even more enticing instrument if a protectionist President is itching to act. It was passed during an era when the US economy was being struck by high inflation and increasing unemployment and faith in free trade on Capitol Hill was waning. It has a series of clauses which defer to the President to take action if needed to react to economic anxiety.

One tool comes in Section 122, the so-called 'Balance of Payments Authority', which permits the President to introduce an additional 15% tariff on imports for 150 days without challenge. He can do so, 'whenever fundamental international payments require special import measures to deal with imports (1) to deal with a large US balance of payments deficit or (2) to prevent an imminent and significant depreciation of the dollar on the foreign exchange markets.'

This could be continued beyond 150 days with the approval of Congress and must be applied to every country. The clause was thus designed to be an across-the-board sanction on trade. The assumption is there would need to be a huge shock that the President suddenly had to cope with, but the wording involved is so sweeping that the latitude of a forceful President is large.

The weaponised sections of the Act are 301(a) and 301(b). Under 301(a), the United States 'must' take action if unfair practices by other trading nations are found to exist. In the case of these 'mandatory' actions, the US trade restrictions must be equivalent in value to the burden of the restrictions being imposed by that country on US commerce. This 'an eye for an eye, a tooth for a tooth' term allows the President to be more selective and surgical than Section 122.

The supplemental Section 301(b) provides appealing discretionary authority to the US Trade Representative, either off their own bat or as the agent of the President, to advance tariff-type measures if an act, policy or practice of a foreign country is found to be unreasonable or discriminatory and it is a burden to US commerce. During the 1980s, even under the nominally 'free trade' Reagan Administration, this provision was often a stick to force others into line.

The US Trade Representative is the beneficiary of a strong hand, if they want to hold it, thanks to the Section 301(b) strictures. That appointee of the President may decide to impose duties or other import restrictions, to withdraw or suspend trade agreements with the nation concerned and/or enter into binding agreements with foreign governments to eliminate the conduct that is in question or to arrange for appropriate compensation. The USTR, whose office was originally established by the Trade Expansion Act of 1962, is a Cabinet-level position which has not really had much prominence within the United States and its apparatus of government, and has very seldom been designated as a foreign policy position of any potency for overseas nations and governments yet, thanks to the 1974 Act and Section 301(b), can be a vital actor in a trade fight.

The final aspect of the legislative tripod is the International Economic Emergency Powers Act of 1977, which was enacted under the Carter Administration with domestic economic distress once again the background and with Congress (heavily under the command of the Democrats in the House of Representatives and the Senate) rapidly becoming disenchanted with free traders.

It was settled upon in part to supersede the Trading with the Enemy Act 1917, which the Nixon White House had taken out of cold storage in 1971. This had been a strategy which even those who cheered the import tariff that it allowed for thought was an innovation of legislative improvisation rather too far and constitutionally deeply dubious.

The Act modernised matters and it commanded that the President had considerable authority to deal with international economic emergencies. Section 1702 is what might be labelled by students of parliamentary statute in the United Kingdom as a 'Henry VIII clause' in its content. It means the President can react to any 'unusual and extraordinary threat' if the President declared that there was a threat that warranted the designation of 'national emergency'. Although there was language which stressed the obligation to 'consult' with Congress, this was not much of a handcuff on a President in a hurry to do something in a certain situation. It was used in connection with both Iran and Nicaragua in the late 1970s but otherwise sat dormant.

As should be clear by now, if a President wants to take US trade policy decisively in a different direction from what (with periodic temporary exceptions) has been considered conventional from Franklin D. Roosevelt to Barack Obama then they will *not* have to solicit new legislation. There is more than enough of it out there. It might well be driving a coach-and-horses through the spirit of what Congress had enacted to turn tariff from a 'beautiful word' to the essence of American international economic thinking, and may not be quite what the authors of the Act involved believed they were delegating to the White House, but the authority is embedded. If Congress does not care for how these laws might be used by Mr Trump in his second term (or as we should really describe it, in the exceptional conditions, as his second first term), then it needs either to repeal the statutes cited here or to draw up a new law to take back control here. The chances that it will do either are slim. The legal status quo is likely to remain exactly as it is.

Added to which, the experience of the first Trump first term, albeit in a haphazard fashion, is more than enough evidence that he will return to this approach again but in a systematic way. His stance on trade in 2016 implied a willingness to reach out for tariffs, but he was not at first surrounded by those who shared his zeal for them. He will not be alone on this one any longer.

In his opening term Mr Trump turned both to Section 232 of the Trade Expansion Act of 1962 and to Section 301(b) of the Trade Act of 1974 and nearly pressed the button on the International Economic Emergency Powers Act of 1977 as well (the Tariff Act of 1930 remained on the shelf).

In 2018, Mr Trump invoked Section 232 to impose tariffs on steel (25%) and aluminium (10%) imported to the United States. These were hardly peripheral materials to target. There were exemptions for Brazil, South Korea, Canada, Mexico and Argentina in return for arrangements being made for quotas and Australia obtained a free pass entirely. The campaign was extended to involve the European Union, Japan and (after Brexit) the United Kingdom as well. It caused a diplomatic and economic stink but his right to function as he did was not plausibly disputed. When the Biden Administration entered office, it did not reverse the Section 232 exercise but struck quota deals with the EU, Japan and UK to soften its effects. The precedent is there.

The President's efforts were not meekly accepted by the international trading community. There was some retaliation which involved unrelated American exports in order to make their point. India, despite ordinarily cordial relations with the Trump White House, was not accepting tariffs without protest. Much of the response by others was aimed at US farmers who suffered an almost instant loss of income. Mr Trump was thus compelled to blow the dust off a Depression-era programme, the Commodity Credit Corporation, to award farmers first up to $12 billion in support and then $28 billion to shore up the heartland as the 2020 election loomed.

The Trump Administration also experimented with Section 301(b) of the Trade Act of 1974. The Office of the US Trade Representative was mandated to start six investigations under the terms of the legislation. Two of them led to tariffs being recommended. The first was with regards to US imports from China due to technology transfer, intellectual property misuse and innovation appropriation and led to $370 billion worth of imports being stuck with tariffs of 25% and 7.5%. This did not go down well in Beijing. The second centred on imports from the EU caused by its subsidies for large civil aircraft, and saw additional tariffs of 15–25% on approximately $7.5 billion worth of imports from the EU. The howls of anguish in Brussels were audible.

At a more detailed level, the USTR commissioned no fewer than 301 investigations into digital services taxes drawn up by a wide range of countries, but Mr Trump left office before any action could be contemplated. During his 2020 campaign it was suggested that the mandatory clauses of Section 301(a) could be activated to allow for blanket tariffs to be minted were he re-elected. His Democratic rivals did not frame much of a response at the time and ex-Vice President Biden felt that he had to sound as committed as the incumbent to preserving US manufacturing jobs.

Finally, Mr Trump toyed with testing how far the International Economic Emergency Powers Act of 1977 could be taken. He threatened to declare an economic emergency involving Mexico and to hand down a universal tariff of 5% on all Mexican goods unless that country did far more to stop illegal migration into the United States across its border. This reflected frustration in the Oval Office that the congressional Democrats had consistently avoided full funding of his vaunted wall. The administration in Mexico City did not want this dispute to escalate further and a package of additional security measures was put together at speed which allowed Mr Trump to claim a win and avoid undermining his own US-Mexico-Canada Trade Agreement.

The idea of this assertive approach has been retained. In one of his last campaign rallies Mr Trump returned to the argument that economic force would compel Mexico to work far harder in stemming the flow of illegal migrants into the United States (even if his contention that Mexico itself could be compelled to finance the wall that would eventually solve the matter was no longer being publicly aired). He could instead raise tariffs by '100% even 200%'. Most of those reading his text did not take this seriously. Those around the new Mexican President – Claudia Sheinbaum Pardo – would not be remotely relaxed about this threat.

The Terms of Trade as well as The Times probably are a-changing. What is to stop this shift? It is clear who would be hurt the most in a trade war. It would not be Washington. In 2022, all trade was 23.1% of US GDP (and 11.6% of GDP was exports). For China the numbers were 37.3% and 19.7%. For France it was 67.6% and 32.7%. Germany a whopping 90.1% and 47.1%. Italy 68.7% and 35%. For the record (with more detail to come in Chapter Twelve), the figures for the United Kingdom are 65.5% and 32.2%.

In theory, Mr Trump could change his mind and deprioritise tariffs as an economic weapon. This seems extremely implausible. His passion for US protectionism is not a novelty.

He has been so firm on the matter that any reversal would be almost impossible to explain away. Some three weeks after his election win, he fired the first shot by warning Mexico, Canada and China of additional tariffs from 'Day One' if they do not increase their co-operation to stop illegal immigration and drugs coming into the US.

Furthermore, as the last chapter observed, if his very substantial tax reductions at home are to be funded by anything other than a scale of additional debt that would make even loyal Senate Republicans anxious, major revenue from tariffs of the kind which the Tax Foundation has (disapprovingly) run its slide rule over is all but compulsory. It has to be presumed that additional tariffs will be an early feature of the restored Trump presidency.

Would Congress offer much resistance? Probably not. The House of Representatives has long been a hotbed of protectionist sympathies. It took epic arm-twisting (and the backing of the House Republican leadership which was in the minority at the time) for that chamber to support the North American Free Trade Agreement under Bill Clinton in 1993 and moving trade deals through the House has become even tougher since then (as the post-Brexit UK may discover). The Democrats are at least as committed to a nationalist stance on these issues as Mr Trump. The Republican presidential victories in the states of Michigan, Pennsylvania and Wisconsin will make Democrats even more wary about looking weak on preserving manufacturing positions. Vice President Harris attempted to rebrand tariffs as a 'Trump Tax' on consumers that could cost the average US family almost $4,000 a year in increased taxes but that line did not carry the day. Even if the Democrats take the House in 2026 (as is expected), they would not be an obstacle to the Oval Office. At most, they may exercise some influence on policy details.

The Senate collectively (if privately) is rather less persuaded by the prowess of protectionism. Its members serve six-year terms so can stand back a touch from the heat of the moment on controversies such as these and serve as a restraining in-fluence (although perhaps not for the one-third of Senators who will be up for re-election in November 2026). The upper house could use confirmation hearings and other means to let those who will serve President Trump over trade know that they might curb his crusading spirit. This will surely fall on deaf ears. The three key laws which a new administration can reach for do not allow for a unilateral senatorial veto. The intellectual distaste that some Republican Senators will hold about protectionism is not a block on a tariff agenda.

Nor should the courts be thought of as some sort of back-stop. The Supreme Court has over many years been permissive about the decision of Congress to delegate trade authority to the White House and has shown no interest in throwing out even dubious instances of presidential power in this realm (such as the Nixon gambit in 1971, sustained by *Yoshida v United States*).

The bulk of case law remains in Mr Trump's favour. This is true be it historic classic arguments such as *US v Curtiss-Wright Export Co* in 1936 and *Maple Leaf Fish Co v United States* in 1985 or what can be rationally inferred from much more recent opinions such as *Loper Bright Enterprises v Raimondo* in 2024. The 'Trump Court' (although all nine justices would hate it called that) will be compliant.

Big business might make some noise and attempt through the Treasury and the Department of Commerce to make vocal representations. Yet, the business lobby in the United States is often fragmented and differing factions will have vastly varying shades of outlook on trade policy. Corporation executives will probably conclude that this is a lost cause and try to work around it. Foreign governments are not likely to be any more effective as they are seen as vested interests.

Which simply leaves American public opinion itself as the potential complicating factor for a tariff-based approach to international economics. The candid fact is not that many electors care, Mr Trump is not subject to consulting the electorate ever again, and the sectors which could be hurt by retaliatory countermeasures (like farmers) are small in number and as before can be financially soothed if they suddenly find the market for their products has closed. There is, in summary, not much to stop what will be a seismic change in trade from happening.

CHAPTER EIGHT

TRUMP AND EUROPE

*The EU and NATO will have to adapt the
most to a new Administration in Washington*

The definition of Europe has long been elusive. Precisely what its boundaries should be thought to be is often a matter of dispute. For the purposes of this analysis, in most sections 'Europe' will be taken to be based on the European Union (so excluding the United Kingdom where the Trump Effect will be examined in a separate chapter). The references to the importance of the decisions that the Trump Administration might make in relation to Ukraine and the war that has raged on its soil since 24 February 2022, involves a country that is not part of the EU (although it would want to be admitted as soon as possible), but plainly is European. There is also an element of complexity in describing the European component of the North Atlantic Treaty Organization (NATO) in that there are major players within it who are not EU members – Turkey and since 2020 the UK – and the occasional EU member which remains outside of NATO, such as Ireland. As a rule of thumb, nevertheless, for most of the issues which will be set out here and which will be of huge significance to the continent of Europe from 2025 to 2029, Europe today equals the EU.

There are at least five domains (one could easily produce a list which included many more) in which the arrival of a restored and revived Trump Administration will cause issues for Europe.

The first is in the merit seen or not in multilateralism in international diplomacy or engagement. The EU is the multilateral entity par excellence. There is nothing quite like it anywhere else in the world. Its internal operations are inevitably multilateral but with examples where unanimity is either formally required for decisions to be made, or much sought after if humanly achievable, and others where qualified majority voting has become the standard means of doing business. Most major foreign policy matters are much closer to the unanimous end of this spectrum as they involve commitments which are potentially central to national sovereignty and interests. The painstaking quest to find the lowest common denominator for an agreement to act often seems a curse.

Even Americans who are sympathetic to the EU and the European ideal struggle to understand it. Confusion is unavoidable to a degree. The EU is obviously far more than a confederation or a loose association of otherwise entirely independent countries, but it remains some way short of a body which could properly be described as a United States of Europe, even of a devolved nature. In some areas it resembles the early United States itself between 1776 and 1789, or even in the half-century or more beyond the adoption of the American Constitution achieved in 1789. There are aspects of EU law which are more driven by the political institutions of Brussels (and Strasbourg and Luxembourg) than is constitutionally permissible in the United States, but other examples where the US has a more centralised structure of administration than seen in the EU.

In any case, because of its divided and fragmented character,

Europe and the largest members of the EU have more chance of punching at or above their weight in a multilateral context than they do if the United States – as the largest single force on the global stage – allows it. A disengaged United States, let alone either an isolationist or unilateral America, is bad news for Brussels as well as Berlin, Paris or Rome (although the current Italian government and its Prime Minister have rather less cause to be disheartened by Trump II than most of their contemporaries).

An important illustration of why multilateralism means so much more to Europe/EU than others is in the G7 set of nations (the G8 before Russia was discarded in 2014 for annexing Crimea).

The EU was first invited to attend what evolved into the G7 in 1977 (when Roy Jenkins was the President of the European Commission) and has been a full attendee at the annual summit since 1981 (so becoming its unstated eighth member, the ninth when Moscow was involved) since that moment. It has all the rights and obligations of being part of this potentially pivotal organisation except that as it is not a country as such it can neither host nor chair a meeting. Being the EU, where internal institutional status is a privilege that is guarded ferociously, it is ordinarily represented of late not by one politician but two, the President of the EU Commission and the President of the EU Council (the leader of the nation that is holding the chair which rotates among the EU member states every six months). This is cumbersome but it still means that Europe makes up courtesy of France, Germany and Italy as individual members, and the EU as a collective one, half of the G7 overall (and was a majority of that body until the UK left the EU).

This is only really worth something if the G7 itself is worth something. The same is true of the G20, the World Bank, the

IMF, the United Nations, the OECD and a host of other alliances. One of the abiding picture episodes of the first Trump term in office was him seated at a table while Angela Merkel, the Chancellor of Germany, appeared to be leading all the rest in surrounding the President asking him agree to something which he looked disinclined to accept. What it was and whether he was convinced to compromise is unclear but the G7, the closest that the world now has to a co-ordinating economic and political establishment, will only be of much utility to the US if Mr Trump continues at least to participate in it, even if he does not see it as constraining his decisions. If the US withdraws more emphatically from multilateral structures this time than it did between 2017 and 2021, then it will be Europe/the EU that is the more diminished.

The second aspect has some overlap, in that it is one where international collaboration is even more essential to Europe/ the EU (but not as crucial to the United States). Europe is the fastest warming continent in the world. Extreme weather episodes (such as those in Spain in late 2024) are becoming more commonplace. Concern about climate change has hence been far more intense in many European democracies than has been witnessed elsewhere. It has also been the catalyst for more political activism but that is an activism that requires almost complete international commitment if it is to be effective. The Paris Climate Accords were signed by all but three eligible nations on 22 April 2016. In advance of it, the EU had been the first major economy to submit its international contribution to the new agreement, which it did in 2015. It ratified the Paris Agreement with some considerable ceremony in 2015. It is a central priority.

It has also led EU member states individually and as a set overall to make big commitments. The largest single one (but there are many) is a law approved by the European Parliament in 2020 that sets supremely ambitious greenhouse gas emissions reduction targets for the year 2050 with the obligation in the comparatively near future (2030) to slash greenhouse gas emissions by 55% of their 1990 levels. Just how much money this will cost is not easy to calculate but it will not be a cheap exercise. Reaching Net Zero by 2050 and then easing emissions downwards from that date involves some truly heroic behavioural assumptions and very deep pockets as well and is really credible only if all governments sign up to the pain, rather than take their own path. In 2020, although it was something of a stab in the dark as a statistical endeavour, the EU had predicted that extra investment of around 260 billion euros a year, or about 2% of the EU GDP, would need to be spent every single year for a decade if the 2030 strictures were to be met.

Under the Biden Administration and its version of a Green New Deal, Europe and the US were on the same track, if not proposing to move forward at exactly the same speed or in entirely the same way. The EU had taken a more prescriptive approach with regard to targets for 2030 not only of greenhouse gas reductions but the proportion of energy which comes from renewables, energy efficiency across the board and the phased elimination of all automobiles that depend on the internal combustion engine rather than electricity, as a matter of legal compulsion. Whereas the US – in part because Mr Biden found that his political programme in this space, including the vital Inflation Reduction Act 2022, was contingent upon maverick Democratic Senator Joe Manchin from the coal-producing state of West Virginia – was more inclined to work with incentives and inducements, rather than the full double-barrel of the law. Had she been elected President, Vice President Harris would have been even more sympathetic to aligning the United States with Europe on climate.

This is clearly off the cards now. The United States will not only depart from the Paris Accords (as it did when Mr Trump was first in the White House) but is even more unambiguous in its dissent from what is considered to be total scientific orthodoxy and political consensus inside Europe (although this is starting to fray on the centre-right of politics in the EU as well). If the United States does not intend to impose targets (if in a less rigid manner than in Europe) and is unwilling to endure the expenditure and inconvenience of transforming its economy to satisfy the demands of the Net Zero mission, then an enormous disparity of approach and attitude will have materialised.

As the incoming Trump Administration is determined to repeal as much of the Inflation Reduction Act as it possibly can (with the green tax credits top of the list to be recycled for a set of alternative tax cuts as described in Chapter Six), there is a fork in the road. Europe (notably the EU) has to determine whether it will proceed without the US for at least four years and has to ask itself whether China and India can be expected to adhere to the letter of the Paris Accords and the urgency of the Net Zero timetable if the US will be abstaining from it. These are likely to be awkward times for an environmental lobby that had seemed to be strong.

The third area for angst for Europe (and the EU as an institution) relates to the international economy and the drive for higher tariffs which a Trump II America looks very likely to embrace.

The European Union is extremely exposed on these matters (although it has hardly been averse to protectionism itself if the mood took it, with successive French Presidents as unapologetic in defence of their concept of the national interest as Mr Trump is accused in Europe of being).

Some basic figures about the EU economy indicate quite how unappealing tariffs would be for Europe. Insofar as there is an 'EU economy' – and one could debate whether adding together a series of what are often rather diverse economies and calling them a whole is compelling (the links between the economic models of Germany, Luxembourg and Bulgaria are not salient) – that economy is the second largest in the world after the United States in nominal terms. The GDP of the EU was assessed at $19.4 trillion in 2024 (about one-sixth of the whole GDP of Planet Earth). With a population of 450 million (a lot more than the US), this suggests a notional GDP per capita of a shade over $43,000 (even the poorest of the American states, Mississippi, would fare well in any comparison with many European countries). The currency of the EU, the euro, has in not much more than two decades become the second largest reserve currency across the globe.

The EU is also, particularly compared with America, an open economy for which trade with others well outside of its jurisdiction is of phenomenal economic importance. It has an economy with a bias towards services at almost 65% but with manufacturing still important at almost 24% (and it remains a core component of the German economy, the biggest in the EU). Agriculture is a meagre 1.5% but counts politically for more than that, such is the need for food security.

China has overtaken the United States as the EU's primary trading partner (and by some distance) but it imports almost twice as much from that country as it exports to it. This is not true for trade with the United States. In 2021 (the last year for which completely accurate information is available), the value of EU imports from the US was some 232,454 million euros (or 11% of the overall total) while the sum of EU exports to the US was 399,391 million euros (18.3% of the entire tally). The EU therefore ran a trade surplus (or the

US a trade deficit) of almost 169,000 million euros and as EU trade with the US has been expanding of late this figure has been steadily increasing. The prosperity of Europe depends heavily on US trade.

As the biggest exporter in the world (allowing for the slightly contestable idea of there being an EU economy, but it is unquestionably a trading bloc with an internal market and its customs union), Europe is not well situated if a trade conflict with the United States over tariffs starts. A universal tariff of even 10%, never mind the higher 20% number that is now more often being mooted, would be extremely consequential, even devastating in some quarters. What to do in response would be problematic. The EU could retaliate (it might sense that it had no choice on the issue) but it is plainly at a disadvantage as the disparity between its imports from and exports to the US is such a chasm. Nor would any notion of parking the US as a trading partner and looking for some other source of business pass muster in boardrooms across the continent. Too much of what Europe exports to the US in services and manufacturing is of the very highest value level.

While China would be the most important target for a Trump-directed Office of the US Trade Representative (because it is a political and economic rival to the United States in a way that the fragmented and humble EU could never be), the European Union would be in the US line of sight. One of Mr Trump's first enquiries when being prepared to meet the leader of any nation, it has been reported, is whether the country involved runs a trade deficit or a surplus with the US. Those at the helm of large EU member states as well as the EU itself will not enjoy such a chat.

The remaining two predictable sectors of contention (although there are plenty more that could be included in the roster) are in essence those of a military, not an economic, kind.

They were fused together in the Republican Party Platform adopted at its 2024 Convention.

The final chapter of that (fairly short) publication, called 'Return to Peace through Strength', a vocabulary that deliberately had echoes of the Reagan presidency, contained these words:

> Republicans will strengthen Alliances by ensuring that our Allies meet their obligations to invest in our Common Defense and by restoring Peace to Europe.

This sentence requires an element of translation to comprehend its significance for Europe.

The words 'restoring Peace to Europe' actually mean ending the current active level of economic and military support that the Biden Administration has offered to Ukraine so that it can at least hold off Russia, and instead pressing Kyiv to enter a negotiated settlement with Vladimir Putin which will inevitably involve territorial concessions and possibly also political reassurances to Moscow that Ukraine would not align itself wholesale to the Western sphere.

The words 'ensuring that our Allies must meet their obligations to invest in our Common Defense' in effect indicates that the extent of the continued US commitment to NATO will be contingent on a strikingly different formula for funding the US presence in Europe. A switch to spending 2.5% of GDP on defence is likely to be the minimum acceptable figure for Mr Trump.

There is in fairness to him a robust case that many European countries have been more than willing to allow the US to pay considerably more than its proper share towards what is, ultimately, the security of the European continent, not that of the United States itself. At the moment, only 23 out of 32 NATO members reach the relatively miserly standard of expending 2% of GDP on their defence. Only Poland and Latvia spend a higher proportion of their GDP on it than the US. It may come as a big shock to many nations to find out how much larger the future invoice for the military is likely to be. This in turn will have a hefty impact on national budgets and economies.

The Trump Effect in both the Ukraine conflict and the integrity of NATO will be as weighty in its own degree as it will be on multilateralism, climate change and the expectant surge in tariffs.

The EU has not been an invisible player since the Russian invasion of Ukraine in February 2022. Huge sacrifices have been made in terms of humanitarian assistance (including to millions of displaced individuals and families) and softening the enormous economic burden on Kyiv. This has continued even as the conflict itself has tended towards stalemate on the battlefield. In October 2024, as an example, the EU adopted yet another package of assistance for the authorities in Ukraine involving an exceptional macro-financial loan of up to 35 billion euros which will be financed by creating a means to monetise the immobilised Russian assets in the EU. This is an imaginative attempt to keep Ukraine afloat without risking sinking the EU's taxpayers.

What Ukraine desperately requires to endure, practically, is guns rather than butter and the forms of weapons system that would most efficiently repel the Russian assault on its people. By the time of the US election of 2024, Russia had (on top of incorporating Crimea 10 years ago) annexed the provinces of Donetsk, Luhansk, Zaporizhzhia and Kherson while Ukraine had made a very much smaller incursion into what had previously been Russian territory as a retaliation acquisition.

This is a notable net loss of terrain, but it would have been far worse without military aid to Kyiv.

The sources of that military assistance (up to August 2024, according to the Kiel Institute) were:

United States $61.1 billion

Sweden $4.6 billion

Germany $11.4 billion

Poland $3.5 billion

United Kingdom $10.1 billion

France $3.4 billion

Denmark $7.0 billion

Canada $2.7 billion

Netherlands $5.5 billion

Finland $2.4 billion

This list of the top ten military supporters of Ukraine is intriguing in many respects. The effort by France, which has an economy almost identical in size to that of the UK, looks unimpressive. Germany has shown some mettle (particularly as how it handles Russia is a matter of serious internal sensitivity) but it has stated that its contribution will be halved during 2025. The smaller countries of Denmark and the Netherlands, some hundreds of miles away from the frontline, seem to have risen to the occasion with some bravado. If the table were based not on the raw sums sent towards Ukraine but on the percentage of national GDP involved, then Poland would be higher up the table still and the Baltic states would be right at the top.

Yet the proverbial 800-pound gorilla is the United States of America. It has put $61.1 billion into the military pot, which is $10 billion more than the next nine contributors added together. Not only that, but the quality as well as the quantity of the military equipment dispatched is of another level compared with anyone else (only the UK comes in at a very distant second on this metric). The impact of the high-technology resources which President Biden provided was, it should be noted, partly blunted by the political restrictions which he imposed on Kyiv, which meant that some of the best assets could not be shot into Russian territory, but with the Biden White House having changed tack once the election was over and released Ukraine to fire ATACMS at Russia, the prospect of President Zelensky making some progress towards expelling Moscow has risen.

The dependency of Ukraine on the US is a weakness as well as a strength. If Mr Trump is determined to cut off that flow of arms to Kyiv, then there is no replacement for it. If he presses Kyiv for concessions to bring the war to a conclusion, then Ukraine will look to Europe and the EU high command for solidarity. Some excruciatingly painful decisions will be needed.

The imbalance that has been demonstrated in Ukraine applies to the final open nerve that is NATO. Mr Trump has never been an enthusiastic supporter of the organisation. In his first run for President, he condemned it as 'obsolete' and an outrageous arrangement for the US to finance. He has offered the impression that he would rather not be at NATO summits, and it remains to be seen if he is prepared to attend in the future or will send a message by his very conspicuous absence that sweeping reform is essential.

NATO is, on paper, a multinational institution with 32 members (all but the US and Canada in Europe) and cumulatively has 3.5 million soldiers and personnel at its disposal. This is in many ways misleading. It suggests a more equal relationship between the US and Europe than is the reality of boots on the ground. The United States is a global superpower (in terms of its reach very much the only country that can be designated as such) and it has a military capacity and a series of commitments that expand far beyond the continent of Europe (although Mr Trump does not want to subsidise many of these other arrangements to the present extent either). In NATO, it is a giant surrounded by pygmies. The US had in 2024 a GDP which was equal to all the other 31 members (Sweden is the most recent recruit) combined and its expenditure on defence was two-thirds and more of the entire NATO number. There remain 85,000 US troops in Europe. There are no European troops in the United States in order to aid the defence of the US.

The Trump Effect on NATO for Europe is much more than an inconvenience. The days of setting low targets for defence spending (and either missing them or engaging in accounting tricks to match them) will surely soon be over. If not, although the President does not have the exclusive legal authority to withdraw the US from NATO or shutter down the structure of it (Mr Biden ended any uncertainty on that account by nudging Congress into passing a law which rendered explicit that no such unilateral action on NATO membership could be undertaken by the Chief Executive), an aggrieved Trump Administration could engage in the equivalent of working to rule within NATO. As insurance on this, perhaps, in late 2024 NATO opted to place Mark Rutte, the former Dutch Prime Minister, who was one of the few European leaders to gel with Mr Trump the first time, as its new Secretary-General.

The internal economics and troop numbers inside NATO as

it stands are brutal. It is a US show. It would be more precisely named if it were rebranded AATR (America And The Rest) because that is what it is as a military entity. If Mr Trump soured on it, then it could keep on the initials NATO, but they would have to stand for Needs Another Thirty Others (in its membership). At a time of weak leadership in many of its capitals, Europe has to wake up to this imbalance.

It is not on its own in being unready for how Trump II will change the world. China is as nervous and for equally strong reasons.

CHAPTER NINE

TRUMP AND CHINA

Washington and Beijing: A 'Hot War'?
A 'Cold War'? A 'Cold Peace'?

Few would disagree that the relationship between the United States and China is and will be central to the international order in the years, indeed decades, to come. That is where the consensus ends.

Predictions and expectations about how the two nations will manage their perhaps inevitable rivalry vary enormously. Recent events and statements have led to increasing debate over a direct or 'hot' conflict between the powers in the context of Taiwan, while others have asserted that an overt clash between the US and China is unlikely, but something akin to the Cold War involving the US and the USSR in the 45 or so years after 1945 is highly conceivable. Another school of thought is that the notion of a military confrontation – be it 'hot' or 'cold' – is essentially a distraction from the real nature of their contest, which is economic and technological (and thus more of a 'cold peace'). The core question with the return of Donald Trump in 2025 is what direction he will want events to take.

The Republican stance over China has swung wildly over the decades. In the immediate aftermath of the Chinese Communist Party coming to power in October 1949, the party presented this event as a disaster for which the incumbent Truman Administration was held responsible. The cry was one of 'who lost China?', espoused with fierce force by a young congressman, then Senator, for California called Richard Nixon. The charge was repeated with even more vigour when the new regime led by Mao Zedong intervened in the Korean War, an action that denied the United States outright victory.

For much of the next twenty years, most Republicans strongly supported the Taiwan administration and echoed its assertion that they were the 'real' government of China at the UN and elsewhere.

In 1972, by contrast, matters were turned upside down by now President Nixon's visit to China and rapprochement with Chairman Mao himself. It is hard to determine who was the more shocked by this spectacle, the Chinese Left or the American Right. There remained a notable Taiwan lobby inside of the Republican Party, but it had the feel of yesteryear to it. When President Carter finally recognised the authorities in Beijing as the legitimate rulers of China in 1979, there was no serious prospect of any subsequent Republican President reversing that decision. The die was cast in diplomatic terms.

Relations between the Reagan White House and Deng Xiaoping were cordial. Those between the first President Bush (who had served as the de facto US Ambassador to China in 1974–1975) and the Chinese paramount leader were close (even despite the enormous difficulties that the Tiananmen Square massacre of 1989 presented to both countries). Matters might best be described as being business-like with George W. Bush in the Oval Office (although not a particularly high priority for him, but the US and China were on the same side when it came to Afghanistan and the War on Terror and Beijing had little interest in aligning politically with Saddam Hussein and Iraq). Most Republicans, in so far as they chose to contemplate it, approved of China's embrace of a more market-orientated approach to economics and assumed that rapidly rising prosperity in China would be the catalyst for some eventual political liberalisation. Bashing Beijing was not a theme for Mitt Romney in the 2012 poll.

It was not absolutely clear, therefore, what the approach of Mr Trump would be when he won the 2016 presidential election. It started amicably enough. The President visited China in 2017, and the red carpet (no pun intended) was well and truly rolled out for him. He was hosted within the heart of the Forbidden City itself (an honour never previously bestowed on a US President). He was feted. He appeared to acknowledge and to appreciate the attention. He was flattering about Xi Jinping. There were no pressing political flashpoints that might prompt Washington to reconsider its policies.

Economics turned out to be another matter entirely. When Mr Trump turned his mind to trade and so to tariffs (as set out in Chapter Seven), China was made a case study for a new US assertiveness. More than $350 billion worth of tariffs were slapped on China and a tit-for-tat trade conflict duly followed (with American farmers caught in the crossfire) until an uneasy settlement of a sort was reached in early 2020. It never looked like it would prove durable if Mr Trump won again that year.

What put matters deeper into the freezer was the arrival of COVID-19 from Wuhan, China in late 2019 and early 2020. The effect was transformational. Mr Trump dubbed it 'the Chinese virus' and at times seemed to encourage speculation that the pandemic had not started accidentally in a wet market, as was the official version, but more suspiciously from a laboratory by accident or by design. Travel restrictions were imposed (the number of direct flights between the US and China collapsed and five years later were nowhere near their previous levels) and political dialogue was all but lost.

Yet, despite this, Mr Trump seemed to respect the Chinese leader and to regard him as someone with whom he and the United States could do transactional business if the terms of trade rebalanced. Even in 2020 he mused that he and Xi 'love each other' (it is improbable that the Chinese President would put it in exactly the same way) and in a newspaper interview shortly before the 2024 election, Mr Trump again stated that he had 'a very strong relationship with him'. Mr Biden had been no friend of China as President, overseeing a highly targeted programme of restrictions which aimed to deny Beijing access to the most sophisticated super semi-conductor technology. China complained that it was being contained and that it was more than entitled to advance its own economic interest.

While Mr Trump might have been in two minds about China, the Republican Party overall was not.

In the period that they were out of office in Washington, D.C., most senior Republican figures had hardened their stand on China, and this was reflected in their rhetoric whenever asked to express it. Mr Trump as a candidate largely fell into line with this but with the caveat that if returned to the White House his own perceived strength and unpredictability would make China more amenable.

The new Republican orthodoxy on China went beyond the trade tensions and tariffs of 2018–2020.

The emerging doctrine, which provided the backdrop for the Republican takeover of government, has been established and articulated by a wide swathe of its foreign and security policy thinkers. To condense and simplify what is close to an internal consensus now, it has six main strands within it.

First, that China is more than a 'competitor' or a 'rival' to the United States (terminology that many within the Biden

117

Administration would also have been at ease with): it is an existential 'threat'.

Second, the above conclusion should become the central operating principle for US foreign policy or, as Mike Waltz, a key adviser to Mr Trump and the incoming National Security Adviser, has written, the US should urgently bring the conflicts in Ukraine and the Middle East to a close so that it can 'finally focus strategy attention where it should go, countering the greater threat from the Chinese Communist Party'. This is a much more holistic view of the US and world order than it was before.

Third, an economic approach based on 'de-risking' China (the formula that the Biden White House and State Department settled on and which the European Union was content to echo) is not enough. A much more far-reaching 'decoupling' of the interdependent US and Chinese economies is wanted (a tall order when the two countries concerned are massive trade partners and 40% of global GDP).

Fourth, the United States must soon regain an overwhelming technological advantage over China. A critical aspect of this would be to prompt (all but compel) the onshoring of semiconductor factories.

Fifth, a large boost in military spending specifically to contain China should be a national imperative (the cost of which could be controlled by insisting that allies pay up more for their own defence).

Finally, the loyalty of others – and their political, economic and military relationship with the US – will be weighted on the extent to which they follow the US lead on China (nowhere for Europe to hide).

This transformed approach and agenda was hammered home in the Republican Platform for 2024.

In Chapter Five, namely 'Protect American Workers and

Families from unfair trade', it asserts that:

'Republicans will revoke China's Most Favored Nation status, phase out imports of essential goods and stop China from buying American Real Estate and Industries.'

Such a strategy, if the US Senate will assist it, radically reverses the US position of the past 25 years.

This was buttressed by the pledge made elsewhere to introduce a 60% tariff on imports from China (much higher than for any other country) with Chinese electric vehicles apparently first in line (they were referred to, often contemptuously, by Mr Trump at rallies, particularly in the state of Michigan). A tougher language about China was also a feature of his acceptance speech at the Convention and (although it was not laboured on long) in his debates with President Biden and Vice President Harris. If words alone are considered to be the currency of politics, then a rollercoaster ride beckons here.

So, what is likely to be the defining feature of the relationship under the Trump II Administration?

The critique which provides the basis for the 'hot war' argument is as follows. China, it is said, has a limited window of opportunity in the second half of this decade at which moment it will have the military capacity to launch a full-scale invasion of what it sees as a 'renegade province'. After that point, Taiwan will have improved its defensive capabilities to an extent that it cannot be conquered.

Even allowing for the further advance of the Chinese military over the next few years, the task of invading and then occupying Taiwan (rather than simply seeking to obliterate it) is an incredibly challenging one. The practical constraints are considerable and essentially render the notion of a swift and surgical strike to be something close to inconceivable. The factors that matter include the following.

The sheer distance involved. At its narrowest point, the

Taiwan Strait is 128 km (79.5 miles) wide, itself a sizeable distance to travel. When realistic embarkation and disembarkation points are taken into account, the sea voyage required becomes at least 50% longer still. The notion that an invasion could be conceived secretly or by stealth lacks any kind of credibility.

The preparation that would be required for such an undertaking would be huge and involve many months of planning and moving the relevant supplies into position. It would be close to impossible to avoid such activity being detected in advance, with Taiwan and its allies able to anticipate what might be directed at them. The idea that it would be possible to disguise all or part of this war effort as a 'military exercise' verges upon the ludicrous. It would need to be the longest 'military exercise' ever recorded. Real intentions would be signalled.

The waters concerned include numerous well-fortified islands between China and Taiwan that are home to an array of extremely effective watching and warning facilities which would enable an attack to be observed and obstructed well before Taiwan itself was struck. The odds on Beijing just orchestrating an attack which had a genuine sense of surprise are about zero.

Any actual invasion would require a vast and slow-moving fleet transporting a minimum of 300,000 troops (more plausibly double or triple that number). The force would have to be much larger still if it were not possible to use the facilities at ports captured largely intact in Taiwan in order to ensure the necessary supply lines back to mainland China. This creates the paradox that destroying critical Taiwanese assets would complicate any military incursion.

Taiwan has few beaches (the maximum figure is only 14 of them) which would be suitable for any amphibious landings to allow incoming troops to establish a viable base on the island.

Taiwan also has an unusual topography which affords it additional security. It has a heavily forested mountain ridge which runs down almost the whole length of the right-hand side of the island for 395 km (245 miles). Cities are spread out around this ridge in a fashion that is close to a natural defensive barrier. This makes conquest of the entire territory exceptionally difficult and would probably require intense urban warfare of a street-by-street character of which the People's Liberation Army has no experience whatsoever, while the defenders of this terrain, albeit outnumbered, would have the seminal asset of intense local knowledge.

Taiwan has developed its own state-of-the-art offensive weapons. It has an impressive air force which can operate using tunnels cut into mountains and which is supplemented by its own satellite systems and ultra-sensitive radar. Controlling the skies over the island by knocking out the Taiwanese air defence system would be an exceptionally ambitious escapade.

All of the above assumes that Taiwan would be on its own in any confrontation with China. It is far more probable that the United States, and even Japan, would feel compelled to intervene in a war. Mr Trump might loathe such an entanglement, but the notion of sitting on the sidelines or of relying entirely on sanctions and tariffs as an American response would be deemed feeble on his own side.

The American presence in this part of the Pacific Ocean is stunning. The US Seventh Fleet is located at Okinawa, Japan. This facility contains 32 separate bases, a large air fleet, 20,000-plus US marines, at least one aircraft carrier strike group (and often two of them) and several cruise missile submarines. This by itself is a formidable armada and one which

China would have to calculate would respond. If Japan were to enter the strife, the fourth largest navy in the world would also be engaged in Taiwan. Outside the wayward North Korean regime, China could rely on few regional allies of any value to it.

The cost of any conflict, while obviously transformational for Taiwan, would be staggering for China.

Military losses would be really massive and a seismic shock for a country which has not been in a significant conflict since it raided Vietnam in 1979 (and was forced back behind its borders). The danger of outright dissent against the Communist Party leadership would be sizeable.

The economic fall-out would be on an epic scale. The best estimates are that China's GDP would shrink by between a quarter and a third in a very short order of time. This is without the full impact of sanctions against its exports which would surely result from any invasion.

The diplomatic and reputational damage to China as it aspires to present itself as a crucial player in global politics would be ruinous. The costs of a conflict far outweigh any benefits. That would remain true even if Taiwan could be totally subdued (which is itself doubtful).

If a 'hot war' is avoidable, then the idea that we are heading for a repeat of the old Cold War might have an enticing logic to it. The term 'Cold War' is, at one level, flexible enough to cover any variety of antagonism that might be witnessed between the United States and China. Yet if it is to imply an international order broadly the same as that of the US and the Soviet Union then it is badly flawed.

The distinctive features of the Cold War (a term first put in the public domain by George Orwell in 1945) include the following three conditions:

- A clash and contest of belief systems (capitalism versus communism as social structures).
- A struggle between superpowers both of which had achieved truly global military reach.
- The mutual possibility of absolute nuclear annihilation by either side of the other.

Where the world is now – and likely to be for an extended period of time – is quite different to this.

The US-China relationship is not a clash and contest of belief systems. In both countries, nationalism is a more important factor than was true of the US–USSR era. Washington is more likely to talk in terms of 'American values' than the virtues of capitalism as such and free market idealism is not what it once was (especially inside the Republican Party, which has strayed from the Reagan model). China's notion of 'market socialism' (with a lively internal argument about the balance between the 'market' and the 'socialism' aspects of it, currently moving away from the former to the latter) is not really being offered or presented as an export to other countries. Indeed, the consistent aspect of the Chinese Communist Party's outlook is an emphasis on the vital 'Chinese characteristics' of its methodology. Whereas Soviet Communism regarded itself as something with universal qualities ripe to be adopted across the planet, China tends to stress the unique elements of its political approach.

It is in terms of 'global reach', however, that any concept of a Cold War II falls apart. The US has a global reach in military terms. China is still striving to secure regional authority in its neighbourhood.

This can be seen in a few basic comparisons between the military capacities of the two countries.

While China's spending on defence has increased markedly

over the past 20 years and today as a percentage of GDP outstrips the US, in absolute dollar terms (at $230 billion) it is still well under a third of that of the current United States military budget (at over $800 billion).

Although China is often described as having 'the largest navy in the world', which it does do strictly speaking (about 355 vessels to 295 for the United States), the statistic is misleading. Having lots and lots of comparatively small boats does not constitute a 'global reach'. It is far better to have a smaller number of larger ships to realise that end. China has two aircraft carriers (with three more under construction). The United States Navy has eleven of them, with two more near completion and an additional seven in the pipeline. In terms of overall tonnage (2019 figures), the US ranks first with some 4,635,628 tonnes. China comes in second with a relatively modest 1,820,222 tonnes. The US Navy has a larger tonnage than the next ten fleets combined. There is simply no competition here in terms of global power. All of this will be reinforced robustly by the recent Australia–UK–US (or Aukus) alliance which will allow Australia, in particular, to play a critical supporting role in the Pacific Ocean.

It is a similar story and ratio when it comes to combat aircraft. The US (in 2020) had some 2,407 such planes at its disposal. China had 922. The US Airforce also had assets with a much longer range than those of China and which could operate with a much larger firepower.

Only when it comes to the armies of the two countries does China (superficially) have a lead. The People's Liberation Army is approximately 975,000 individuals strong, more than twice the size of the regular US Army (about 480,000 persons). The difference, though, is that 99% of the PLA is located within China, responsible for 22,117 km (13,743 miles) of borders with 14 nations. The United States Armed

Forces (the Army plus other services) are everywhere.

Everywhere really means everywhere. It is the vast Grand Canyon in terms of overseas bases between the US and China which hammers the nails in the coffin of a Cold War comparator. The United States has at least 750 bases internationally. China has, depending on what you regard as an overseas base, one, two, three, five or eight such bases. Why the uncertainty?

The only absolutely unambiguous Chinese overseas base is in Djibouti in the Horn of Africa. Beijing is supposedly erecting a building at the Ream base in Cambodia on a 25-year lease, but what exactly it is remains unknown (and the Americans have an outpost at the same place anyway). Some sort of construction is also occurring in Tajikistan but so close to the Chinese border that it is rather stretching the idea of an overseas base to its limits. There are five other (small) examples of China having created man-made bases in either disputed or international waters close to its own coastline. If you just count the ones which most bodies agree were definitely not in an area which China could legitimately argue was its water, the overall number of 'overseas' bases makes five. Accept all of them as outside China, then it is eight. Any attempt to equate US–China today with the old US–USSR era starts to look surreal.

Furthermore, this is not a competition in which one could expect China to 'catch up' swiftly. To be of any serious utility, an overseas base needs to be one where (a) there is a stable and sympathetic host country and regime (b) there is significant strategic worth and (c) the location fulfils a military need (so deep-water ports for a navy to be located). The supply of such assets internationally is finite, and the US already has the pick of the planet.

Finally, in terms of the crude currency that is nuclear weapons and the prospect of Armageddon, this is not the

Cold War Revisited either. The US hold, on the most recently available data, a stockpile of 5,428 nuclear weapons of which 1,644 are actively deployed (on a missile so ready to go if required). China has between 350 and 400 in total, most of which are submarine-based, so perhaps about half of them are actively deployed (and with a much more limited range than their US counterparts). On a day-to-day basis, France, with 280 actively deployed nuclear weapons, commands a bigger arsenal.

The concentration on the military dimension of US–China competition thus appears misplaced. The real contest is economic, and more precisely which country dominates key technologies in the future. All of the analysis above relates to conventional and highly visible military hardware which could, as some senior military analysts have speculated, be rendered almost redundant if one or other of the two nations acquires a unique dominance as a cybersecurity superpower. This is the concern that motivates the Pentagon and the CIA the most (their equivalents in China are no less concerned about finding themselves exposed as a modern version of Mao's 'Paper Tiger').

This has become more transparent as the Chinese economic model has changed under Xi Jinping and it started to do so before COVID-19 arrived as a factor. The formula which China had followed for the better part of 40 years from 1978 onwards had placed a premium on the highest possible level of economic growth by the most direct route open to it. This had meant, in practice, becoming a mass manufacturer of comparatively low-value goods at enticing prices for export to the developed world.

This strategy had been seen as an outstanding success until the last decade or so, when it came to be reassessed. The by-products which it created, such as the emergence of a celebrity capitalist class (or 'Jack Ma syndrome'), rising economic, social, and regional inequality and a reliance on others for the imports of technological building blocks (such as semiconductors) are now seen as undesirable. Under President Xi, the private sector will be closely monitored by the State (and hence the Party), rampant capitalist excesses will be curtailed, and technological self-sufficiency is an essential target.

This is the shift that will drive fundamental tensions between the US and China, rather than the military sphere.

The US and China have become direct economic competitors in a way they were not before. The US is determined to keep China from making rapid progress towards technological self-sufficiency by restricting its access to outside technologies, be that through overt acquisition or more covert means (including what Washington sees as shameless industrial espionage).

The new 'arms race' does not involve missiles and warships but the command of areas like artificial intelligence, digital science, quantum computing, cybersecurity and biotechnology.

The fundamental impact of the Trump II presidency is that, whether it is his initial intention or not, a cold peace is far more probable than a hot war or a new Cold War. It will fall to him to establish how this is organised, and how it operates on the American side. This will have massive repercussions elsewhere.

CHAPTER TEN

TRUMP AND THE MIDDLE EAST

*Much the same strategy as before but in a far
more sensitive situation*

The United States has not historically been intensely involved in the Middle East as a region. Even in the midst
of World War II, it did not appear a priority engagement. The
Cold War and aspects of domestic politics began to change
matters shortly thereafter. The US was the first nation to recognise the fledgling state of Israel. The Eisenhower Administration in the 1950s effectively obliged Britain and France to
abandon their intervention to seize the Suez Canal (and with
it topple General Nasser in Cairo) for fear that as it smacked
of colonialism it would assist the Soviet Union with Arab
nations. The decision of the United Kingdom to abandon its
formal role in the Persian Gulf from the late 1960s obliged
the US to become the security patron in its stead.

From there on in, intervention became almost automatic
and vital to America's own interests. The Yom Kippur War
of 1973 and subsequent OPEC oil embargo led Henry
Kissinger, the US Secretary of State under President Nixon
(and President Ford), to engage in shuttle diplomacy. After
that moment, the Middle East would become as important to
the US as Europe and East Asia (at times even more so). The
defection of Egypt from the camp sympathetic to the USSR
offered an opportunity which President Carter sought to seize
via the Camp David Agreement. The Iranian Revolution and

allied hostage crisis would prove a bitter blow to that Administration.

The Reagan White House was closely aligned to Israel but focused far more on the Soviet Union. George H. W. Bush brought the United States back in spectacularly through the Gulf War in 1991. His successor but one and son, George W. Bush, responded to the atrocities of September 11 2001, with an incursion in Afghanistan (whether it should be considered part of the Middle East is worthy of discussion) and then the full-scale military drive to enforce regime change in Iraq (a Middle East state most certainly). This proved to have painful aftershocks as seeking a peaceful settlement thereafter would prove exceptionally difficult. As late as 2010, the United States had 100,000 soldiers in Iraq, more than 70,000 in Afghanistan and a host of others in bases across the area. It fell to Barack Obama to scale this back, but it was an episode of many fits and starts. America was to a degree trapped in the Middle East by oil and the risk of terrorism rooted there.

It was this past that constrained Donald Trump as a candidate and as a President the first time. He had oscillated in 2015–2016 between appearing to want to curtail the US armed role in the region and being more assertive in military terms. It was not the only example of inconsistency in thinking and policy, but it mattered more than most did. His record in office is hence very mixed, but it leaves clues as to what might happen from 2025 on.

There are five features of the first Trump Administration in the Middle East worth closer scrutiny.

The first was that, even by the standards of American politics, he was a staunch supporter of Israel and delivered on his promises made in advance of the 2016 presidential election as no figure had done before. The contest for the White House before Mr Trump turned up on the scene had an almost pantomime quality to it, as the aspiring candidates solemnly pledged that they would transfer the US Embassy in Israel from Tel Aviv to Jerusalem but, once they had made their home at 1600 Pennsylvania Avenue, one reason or another would prevent them doing this. Mr Trump, by contrast, stuck with his side of the bargain and was much cheered by Israel and its Prime Minister, Binyamin Netanyahu (a smart and shrewd operator in the US political sphere) for doing so. He would also later recognise Israeli sovereignty over the Golan Heights. They would remain close to the end, although Mr Trump was said to be aggrieved when his Israeli friend recognised the victory of Joe Biden in 2020 and congratulated him on it.

The movement of the US Embassy, which opened in May 2018 on the seventieth anniversary of the foundation of Israel, with no attempt to soften the symbolic force of this shift whatsoever, was not the only instance of Mr Trump acting as neither Mr Obama (who had scant emotional empathy with Israel), or the second Mr Bush (who did connect with the country and its story) or Mr Clinton (in many ways even more a natural ally of Israel than his GOP predecessor or his successor) would choose to do. In his visit to the Middle East in May 2017, Mr Trump became the first US President to appear at the Wailing Wall. He was also openly agnostic as to whether Israel should stop building settlements on disputed territory. The phrase 'two-state solution' for the outstanding Israel-Palestinian stand-off were not words often used by him. In short, as President, Mr Trump was about as intimate a friend as Israel was ever likely to acquire.

This did not mean that 'the art of the deal' was not witnessed elsewhere in the vicinity. As a contender in 2015–2016, Mr Trump had said almost nothing of any detail on Saudi Arabia. The second telling aspect of his tenure was how much more enthusiastic he became in office. The US has been the protector of the Saudis for decades, but it was in the mutual calculation of both sides not to be explicit about how deep these ties drilled down. Not so under Mr Trump.

This manifested itself in several forms. On the same tour which included the Wailing Wall in Jerusalem, the American entourage went on to Saudi Arabia. The Riyadh Summit there with the President and King Salman produced a Vision Statement which went further publicly than the two countries had been comfortable with beforehand. There would be an enormous arms sale totalling $115 billion with the Saudi regime, which in different times Israel might have opposed and mobilised its many supporters on Capitol Hill to scupper. Mr Netanyahu hung back from this. The President (through his son-in-law Jared Kushner, who turned out to be a crucial figure) developed a close association with the Saudi Crown Prince (and the power behind the throne) Mohammed bin Salman, who was heading an imaginative effort to modernise the Kingdom.

This would be a pact which continued despite the storm when Jamal Khashoggi, exiled to the US and a contributor to the *Washington Post*, was murdered in gruesome fashion in the Saudi consulate in Istanbul, Turkey, with the Saudi leadership widely blamed for it. Mr Trump also allowed the Crown Prince a free hand to intervene in the civil war in Yemen, but this would incite a disagreement with Congress, notably the Senate, and a retreat took place. The authorities in Saudi Arabia (as the Prime Minister of Israel did) regretted Mr Trump leaving. The same cannot be said for a string of countries across Europe especially.

Thirdly, a sensational by-product of the emerging understanding with the Saudi leadership was that the United States found itself with an opportunity, initially secretly, to pull off what by any yardstick was a diplomatic coup, completely unexpected when Mr Trump had first become President. The device was what would come to be called the Abraham Accords, and the instigator of it was the first son-in-law Mr Kushner. This was an improbable development for multiple reasons. Mr Kushner held no official office. He had no qualifications to conduct US foreign policy. He is also Jewish, which would render him suspect in certain Arab quarters. The idea that he could broker what past Presidents and secretaries of states could not verged on the laughable.

It turned out that Mr Kushner would be the one who laughed last and loudest. In August 2020 it was announced that Israel and the United Arab Emirates would normalise their relationship. This would be followed by a similar accord between Israel and Bahrain. Morocco and Sudan signed up as well, but they mattered far less as they were not (even on the most expansive of definitions) Middle East actors. The UAE and Bahrain clearly were in that category, and it was absolutely obvious that they would not have entered a dialogue with Israel and settled their differences with the Jewish State if Saudi Arabia had disapproved of such a reconciliation.

This suggested that the Accords might be capable of further extension with Saudi blessing. Kuwait and Oman were possibilities. Qatar, which steers an independent course in the Gulf, probably not. The real bonanza would be if Saudi Arabia itself, the custodian of the Holy Sites of Islam, would also allow for an exchange of ambassadors with Israel as part of a bigger bargain with the United States that would totally cement its own security. This would have seemed a barking mad idea at the beginning of the Trump presidency. It no longer looked insane at all.

The motivations of all concerned were sharpened by the fourth facet of the first Trump era: Iran.

The arrival of Mr Trump in Washington proved an electric shock for the leaders in Tehran. On the campaign in 2016, the aspiring Republican nominee had stated his disapproval of the Joint Comprehensive Plan of Action negotiated between the US, Iran (with which America has not had diplomatic relations since 1979) and five other world powers (including the UK) in 2015. The agreement would exchange an easing of what had proved crippling sanctions against Iran for evidence of progress that Iran's nuclear aspirations were civilian in their form, not military. Or, as many Republicans including Mr Trump said, Iran was being bribed not to build the bomb.

From the outset, Mr Trump considered this a spineless stance. His preferred route was for all of those who had signed up to the scheme promoted by Mr Obama and his Secretary of State John Kerry to wash their hands of it, citing as a pretext that Iran had violated its terms. Proof that this was indeed the case was, alas, not that straightforward to come by. The five allies found alibis not to end the understanding with Iran, whom they preferred to keep inside the tent. The only 'Plan B' that they could spot would involve a proactive military effort to deter Iran.

Irritated by the ambivalence of the five (and cheered on informally by the Saudis, and others at the Sunni end of the Muslim faith), Mr Trump went off unilaterally. In 2018, after almost 18 months of trying to convince partners to come with him, he finally renounced the deal with Iran. In April 2019 he raised the stakes further by officially damning the Islamic Revolutionary Guards Corps as a terrorist organisation and placing personal sanctions on the senior Iranian leadership. His posture would be that of 'maximum pressure' on Tehran in all spheres of activity.

If there was any doubt about what he meant by this then it evaporated in January 2020. Iran had pushed back against the United States by becoming more aggressive in allowing its proxies in the Gaza Strip, Lebanon and the Red Sea to disrupt Israel and the Americans. It considered this to be self-defence. The strategy relied disproportionately on the acumen of one man, General Qasem Soleimani, who was a national hero within Iran; as a consequence, his standing was second only to that of the Supreme Leader himself. He was killed in an American drone strike after landing at Baghdad International Airport on 3 January 2020. This came as a thunderbolt to Tehran (it also made plain how much the authorities in Iraq were collaborating with America's great foe). When Iran threatened revenge for his loss, Mr Trump retorted that he would bomb 52 'very high level and important sites' in Iran if they did anything (one for every US hostage taken in 1979). It can be concluded with confidence that Iran, unlike Saudi Arabia, was glad to see Mr Trump go.

The final component in what amounted to a 'Trump Doctrine' in the Middle East was less one of unilateralism than semi-isolationism. He pursued travel bans against the residents of various nations in the area (but was obstructed by the US judiciary, including Republican appointees). The President did not want to be caught up in wars or conflicts that had no termination date. He would avoid them by backing a strongman who could keep a lid on a country that could boil over, such as President Abdel Fattah El-Sisi of Egypt, who had come to his office through a military coup in 2013 and then dubious elections (Mr Trump welcomed him into the White House, which Mr Obama had always refused to do). In Afghanistan, Iraq and Syria, Mr Trump could blow hot and cold but was instinctively very wary.

This was reflected very starkly in Afghanistan. Before winning the presidency, Mr Trump had been inclined to increase the American military force to contain the Taliban and associates. This did not last long as an idea. By February 2020, he had allowed the US to sign the Doha Agreement, which was a conditional pact with the Taliban which called for all foreign troops to leave Afghanistan 14 months later if the Taliban agreed to certain restrictions on its behaviour (how these were to be enforced once US soldiers had departed was never articulated). When Mr Biden initially extended the deadline to September 2021, the by then ex-President condemned the delay and insisted the US should stick to his schedule. When the US did remove itself from Afghanistan amid scenes of abject chaos in August 2021, with the Taliban walking into authority with all that implied for the status of women and any hint of pluralism in the country, Mr Trump redefined his prior support for the evacuation of troops and slammed Mr Biden for his deeds.

In a similar spirit, although Mr Trump could not entirely end the US military presence inside Iraq (there remain about 2,500 troops there), he did not want them anywhere they might face attack and quickly decided that he would not expend an ounce of political capital on Baghdad politics. The attack on General Soleimani was the final nail in the coffin for US aspirations inside Iraq. It was now to be a place for damage limitation, a long way from the aims of President Bush.

The other instance of 'in then out' was Syria and the civil war that raged against the Assad regime. At first, the recklessness of what was left of the government in Damascus demanded that Mr Trump involve himself with the conflict (which was not his intention). When there was conclusive evidence of a chemical weapons attack at Khan Shaykhun in April 2017, Mr Trump did what all of his predecessors would have done and drew a line in the sand, authorising the US Navy to launch strikes at the Shayrat Airbase under the control of

Mr Assad's operatives. Only two months later, though, the President signed off on a phasing out of the CIA's support for anti-Assad rebels. He later indicated to Turkey that he would not object if it filled the void in the north of Syria (to the detriment of Syrian Kurd fighters, whom Turkey wanted to be rid of). His stealth exit was interrupted by events once more as the Douma chemical weapons assault forced him to endorse a military reaction. He knew where he wanted to be despite this. By December 2018, ignoring resolutions in the Senate and the loss of Defense Secretary James Mattis, he was out. The US would return only briefly in 2019 for raids that led to the deaths of Islamic State leaders.

Trump is now back. By the standards of an unpredictable President, what he will aspire to do in the Middle East is atypically predictable. Mr Trump will stand shoulder-to-shoulder with Israel. He will want to pick up with Saudi Arabia where he left off. Extending the Abraham Accords would be a bonus (but it seems that Mr Kushner will not be returning to Washington, D.C. to assist him). Iran will be Public Enemy Number One in the region. Other firefights will be studiously avoided. His choice for Secretary of State, Senator Marco Rubio, puts the stamp on the Trump II agenda.

The challenge for the ex-President turned next President is that much has happened in the past four years and this may make simply reconstructing where he was before considerably harder.

The first, obviously, is an outright conflict between Israel and Hamas. On the morning of 7 October 2023, apparently without any detection in advance by the normally extremely effective Israeli military and intelligence establishment, Hamas stole into Israel itself, murdering 1,195 Israelis and a clutch of foreign nationals (often by utterly barbaric methods), of whom some 815 could only be considered to be outright civilians, many of whom had the sheer misfortune to be at a music festival close to the border with the Gaza Strip, and seizing 251 people (Israelis and some other nationals, including Americans) to be taken as hostages and to some extent as human shields should Israel (as it would) seek retribution for this attack.

Israel duly invaded Gaza (after earlier and very substantial air strikes) just under three weeks later. What can only be described as a war has been fought on the ground and in the skies ever since. It has no apparent end to it as in these conditions how one declares victory is unclear. The impact on civilians has been exceptionally damaging in human and in material terms. Much of Gaza has been flattened, to the transparent unease of many observers overseas, although US public opinion as a whole has deemed that Hamas and hence Gaza had it coming to them. The exception was the small Arab American community in the United States itself, which was significant in the critical swing state of Michigan and damaged Vice President Harris (Mr Trump abnormally kept his own counsel).

The carnage in Israel/Gaza is a fact on the ground that Mr Trump will inherit, but did not exist in 2017. The United States is already an actor here and that will not be altered after January 2025. In the wake of the 7 October outrage, Mr Biden asked Congress for $14 billion in military aid to Israel and the legislature eventually handed over $19.3 billion in military assistance (and a $9.2 billion humanitarian package for the residents of Gaza itself). The main argument (from the House Republicans) was whether money intended for Ukraine should be diverted to Israel. The smoke-signals from the Trump camp were that this would not be deemed misappropriation.

It would seem that Israel has succeeded in smashing Hamas

as an organisation and a structure. It can no longer function from the many miles of tunnels below buildings that had become its mode. Its political leader, Ismail Haniyeh, was taken out at the behest of Mossad in Tehran itself (a triumph reminiscent of the Steven Spielberg film *Munich*) and its military mastermind Yahya Sinwar, the architect of the 7 October episode, was shot dead in a routine IDF patrol fight.

Hamas and Gaza would be a massive spanner in the works by themselves, but Hezbollah and the Lebanon more than double the difficulty. Hamas (a Sunni Muslim entity) is an adopted child of Iran, one taken in on the 'my enemy's enemy is my friend' dictum. Hezbollah is a proper Shia off-spring. Although it approved of and supplemented the Hamas raid on Israel in October 2023 by a vast rocket attack on the Shebaa Farms and elsewhere, it initially proceeded with caution in not letting itself be drawn into a conflict with Israel, for which neither it nor Tehran was ready.

It could not be half at war with Israel indefinitely. Some 60,000 Israelis had been forced to move out of their homes near the border with Lebanon to take them out of range of missile assaults and to avoid any chance of anything like a repeat of the 7 October debacle in Gaza. The Israeli Cabinet did not feel that it could allow them to be displaced for the foreseeable future. Although a war on two fronts is one which would be approached very carefully as an operation, the direct involvement of Iran in co-ordinating the activities of Hezbollah aggrieved the Israelis dearly.

They have come back with an astounding string of initiatives. In April 2024 an operation struck the Iranian consulate in Beirut and killed a number of senior Hezbollah and Iranian figures. This would be the prelude to a stunning September offensive in which exploding pagers led to the deaths of at least 12 individuals linked to Hezbollah, and injured perhaps thousands more of them, decimated the ability of Hezbollah to communicate within itself and revealed that Israel had acquired a technological edge over its foes which went beyond its renowned expertise in cyberattacks (which had interrupted, along with selective assassination of senior scientists, Iran's efforts to upgrade its nuclear options for more than a decade). A sophisticated bombing enabled Israel to penetrate the inner sanctum of Hassan Nasrallah, the Hezbollah leader who had spent many years whipping up his own adherents and sections of the Lebanese population against the Zionists in Jerusalem and to remove him and a collection of other major colleagues. Decapitation (Israel has always considered the likes of Hamas and Hezbollah to be top-down institutions, where charismatic and technically savvy leaders are immensely consequential) was threatening the credibility of Hezbollah as a viable organisation and putting Iran into its box. In late November 2024, an Israel-Hezbollah ceasefire in Lebanon emerged but it looked like a mere time-out.

None of this had been in the equation when Mr Trump took the Oath of Office in 2017. It will be in 2025. It also led to two direct military conflicts between Israel and Iran, avoided before then. In April 2024, Tehran sent a wave of drones and comparatively slow-moving rockets at Israel itself. With the help of the US military and its own Iron Dome shield, Israel swatted them all away. Washington pressed Israel hard to retaliate in only a minor manner, avoiding either bombing any suspected nuclear sites or oil-production facilities. Mr Netanyahu obeyed his instructions. In October 2024, after the loss of Hassan Nasrallah and as a belated reaction to the assassination of Mr Haniyeh on its own soil, Iran lashed out at Israel for a second time but with more firepower. Some missiles did get through, but the majority of them were taken out and casualties were light. Mr Netanyahu deferred his response and again accepted American demands for restraint (and the US election campaign had not been settled) but showed in what one suspects will be a high impact if low-profile operation that Israel can disarm Iran's air defence system as it wishes. Predictions of Armageddon were wide of the mark, but this is a big powder keg with a short fuse.

Finally, on Thanksgiving Day 2024 (28 November), let alone Election Day 2024 (5 November), absolutely no one thought that the Assad regime in Syria would fall in under a fortnight. This could mean that the powder keg is yet bigger and the fuse is even shorter from now on.

It is also Mr Trump's powder keg once he is back behind his desk in the Oval Office. In the time that he has been away, the number of US troops in the region has risen from 30,000 to 45,000, in places such as Bahrain, Djibouti, Jordan, Kuwait and the UAE. The diplomatic standing of his country in the Middle East has, however, decreased and by some margin. The many trips to the area by Secretary of State Antony Blinken have, if anything, made America look impotent. The Biden Administration decided on entering office to give the Saudi authorities the cold shoulder and as a result saw them co-operate with Vladimir Putin on oil output levels and hence prices in 2022, despite the Russian invasion of Ukraine, then host Xi Jinping of China for a set of summits and then allow Beijing to be the facilitator as it reignited a diplomatic relationship with Tehran. Mr Trump may want to bring the old band back together with the Saudis. What tunes will it play?

The restored Trump presidency will therefore meet a Middle East in which the region itself has become the unpredictable element, not the man himself. It will be a stretch both to allow Israel more scope to deal with its enemies and restore the US as the diplomatic top dog. Mr Trump might have a blueprint for American hegemony here. It may not be realised by him.

CHAPTER ELEVEN

TRUMP AND THE WIDER WORLD

*Where and how the return of the President
will make the most impact*

Europe, China and the Middle East are the areas where the Trump Effect will have the most economic and political force (although in the last case, if experience holds true, the region may be the one that has the most effect on Mr Trump, rather than the other way around). This does not mean that they are the places which will necessarily be seen as the highest or as the most immediate priority for the President himself and many of those around him (let alone in the order that they have been listed here). Together they constitute not much more than a third of the global population (although their collective GDP is rather higher). There are other nations and regions which will be viewed as very urgent to deal with (even if many would say this was misplaced). Another set will have energy and time expended on them in what may prove a shrewd move. There will be areas (including almost an entire continent) which will be ignored.

In one very important regard, the most compelling foreign country for Mr Trump to impose his will upon does not have its capital as Berlin or Brussels, Beijing, Baghdad or Beirut. It is Mexico and Mexico City which matter to an extraordinary degree to him. Mexico is where domestic policy and foreign politics meet and mould. This is because of the stance that Mr Trump, with virtually the whole of the Republican Party now content to be his backing chorus, has taken on border security, illegal migration into the United States and the need for a wall.

The bonds between the US and Mexico could and should extend beyond this single issue. The two countries are, for example, most of the time the largest trading partners with each other. In 2022, the United States exported $276.5 billion to Mexico, and it collected imports worth $384.7 billion from that nation. The fact that this equates to a sizeable trade surplus for Mexico is not a statistic about which Mr Trump has any enthusiasm whatsoever. Then again, of the current top ten US trading partners, it runs a surplus in goods with only one of them (the country will be identified later in this volume). Mr Trump's distaste for these figures led him when first in the White House to name and shame and threaten to invoke tariffs upon those large US companies (including Ford) who had relocated factories south of the border.

It is the border itself that Mr Trump almost single-handedly has placed at the centre of politics. It stretches for 1,954 miles (3,145 kilometres) and touches the states of California, Arizona, New Mexico and Texas. It is only the tenth longest such boundary between two nations seen anywhere in the world, but it is the most regularly crossed international demarcation line on the planet. There is something like 350 million legal and recorded journeys across it each year. At a minimum there are 500,000 successful but illegal one-way trips every twelve months (but that number could be much larger). As the border has been porous for many years now, it is thought that there are at least 11.5 million undocumented workers in the United States (overwhelmingly having entered from Mexico, although the individuals involved might not be Mexicans). Almost seven out of eight of these people are believed to have lived in the US for seven years or more. There are sections of the US and sectors of the economy that have come to depend on them. Although Mr Trump and others denounced them as 'criminals', the proof of this in numbers is not persuasive. The power and evil of the drug cartels in Mexico is another matter.

This has been a sore in American public life since well before Mr Trump entered political life. The first attempt at cutting off the flow through constructing some kind of barrier was made in 2006 at the behest of George W. Bush (a Texan) but his successor (Mr Obama) was less focused on it. The original stretch of the wall (more of a sizeable fence really) covered 600 miles (966 km) or a little under a third of the entire boundary. In his first week as President, Mr Trump would issue Executive Order 13767, which sought to create what he saw as a proper obstruction across the whole US-Mexico border. Congress was unconvinced and impeded him. By the time that he departed the scene in January 2021, he had managed to add only 455 miles (732 km) extra.

It was not for a lack of effort. Mexico felt the heat. The new man in the Oval Office made life very uncomfortable for President Enrique Peña Nieto, who had to fend off the suggestion from Mr Trump that not only would the wall happen but that Mexico City would finance it (one of the reasons why Congress was coy about the idea is that it deemed the official estimate of the cost at $22 billion as vastly below what the expenditure would ultimately be, and no one thought it credible that Mexico would hand over up to $70 billion to erect the mother of all barriers). Mr Trump was not subtle in linking the re-negotiation of the North American Free Trade Agreement (NAFTA), which he was also insisting upon, with Mexico being accommodating on reducing the numbers of illegal migrants entering the US. The big stick of tariffs would be wielded. A toothache in American domestic politics became a massive headache for Mexico.

A different President there – Andrés Manuel López Obrador – did better at either distracting Mr Trump, or soothing his dissatisfaction, or making it look as if meaningful work was occurring. This did not prevent the President putting completing the wall front-and-centre in 2020 as well.

As it has been in 2024. Another Mexican President, Claudia Sheinbaum, not long in her office, is bound to be on the end of a stream of demands from Washington. Mexico is surely in for a rough ride. This time round, Mr Trump is in a stronger position to win the money needed from Congress.

There are not many illegal crossings into the United States from Canada which must be a mercy. It is also a very major trading partner with the Americans (along with Mexico and China) but it runs a goods trade surplus of about $50 billion (approximately half the size of that of Mexico). This was not a cause for contention under President Bush or President Obama. They placed more weight on Ottawa being a congenial neighbour, a reliable ally and the other non-European NATO nation.

Mr Trump was not so relaxed at the first time of asking. He had been in power for three months when he threw himself into a long-standing bilateral trade dispute involving softwood lumber. That spat was still simmering when Canada was struck with tariffs on its aluminium and steel exports to the US, which triggered a retaliation from the Maple Leaf nation. It also faced the inconvenience of NAFTA being killed off, although its replacement in terms of the US and Canada was little different in its deals. It was turbulence regardless. The personal dynamics between Mr Trump and Justin Trudeau, who had become the Liberal Party's Prime Minister in 2015, struck outsiders as less than amicable. Canada remained valuable to US intelligence agencies as part of the elite 'five eyes' arrangement (the US, UK, Australia, New Zealand and Canada) but it was not otherwise considered of any stature to the President or to his State Department.

Whether this holds for Trump II is uncertain. Mr Trudeau has been sailing right next to the rocks at home. He has insisted that he will take the Liberals into an election due in 2025, but his party may determine that someone else is more likely to reduce and ideally reverse what is a massive deficit in the opinion polls. If not, Pierre Poilievre, for the Conservatives, will cope with Mr Trump.

It is a rather random story for the rest of the Americas. In his first term, Mr Trump did not take an intense interest in South America or its national leaders. He made an exception to this rule for President Jair Bolsonaro of Brazil, whom he aligned as a personal and philosophical ally. President Bolsonaro was received with pomp and ceremony at the White House and flattered with the declaration that Brazil was to have the accolade of a 'major non-NATO ally' and that Washington would support its bid for OECD inclusion. No such attention was lavished on the Presidents seated in Argentina or Chile, let alone more modest nations such as Ecuador, Columbia and Peru (not that many previous American Presidents have broken much political sweat for them either). The Caribbean was completely irrelevant, other than having the dignity of the likes of Haiti dismissed in a leaked conversation between Mr Trump and a stunned set of congressmen as 'sh*tholes'.

Those marked down as undesirables in the Americas were, in the first Trump term, left aware of their status. The Trump White House imposed sanctions on President Daniel Ortega and his acolytes in Nicaragua. Cuba, which Mr Obama had sought some reconciliation toward, would be firmly restored to the cold. The US took a tougher line on Venezuela, with

President Nicolás Maduro condemned and shunned and the opposition leader, Juan Guaido, recognised as the Acting President instead. The three nations were slammed as the 'troika of tyranny' by John Bolton during his brief, and, from the tone of his memoirs, deeply unsettling time with Mr Trump.

The second Trump tenure will probably be very similar but with one major twist. With Luiz Inácio Lula da Silva back in and Mr Bolsonaro on the sidelines, Brazil will cease to be favoured. Mr Trump's new best friend in South America is destined to be Javier Milei, the chainsaw-loving libertarian economist who has become the President of Argentina. His invitation to the White House will not take long to be in the post. Most of his fellow leaders will be lucky to get more than the odd word at the margins of any international events and summits that they might attend.

That will also be the fate of another numerically sizeable series of countries and leaders who will be lucky if they figure on the foreign policy radar screen of Republican Washington. Africa as a whole, but Sub-Saharan Africa in particular, appears to have been of no interest to either the President as a person or, beyond the lowest common denominator of diplomacy, those who toiled on his behalf in the State Department (Mike Pompeo was willing to be seen in Africa on occasion). The only issue in which the White House intervened was on behalf of Egypt (strictly speaking within Africa but of importance to the US as part of the Middle East instead), which, along with Sudan (which had secured points by signing up to the Abraham Accords) became embroiled in a dispute with Ethiopia over its Grand Ethiopian Renaissance Dam plan. Uncle Sam was commissioned to side with the President of Egypt in a menacing manner. This seemed to have some effect (although the disagreement is not completely settled). This was unusual. Africa was marginalised as it had been before Mr

Bush and Mr Obama looked at it. There are robust grounds for anticipating that it will be rendered invisible again under Trump II.

The challenge of China, and the dedication that many in the new Administration will have to containing and then curtailing it as an alternative dominant nation to the United States, means that East and South Asia will come to the attention of many advisers around the President, even if he himself, beyond economics and trade, is probably less driven by casting China in chains.

Which could be a mixed outcome for Japan and South Korea, the most significant other actors in the East Asian theatre. Japan is undoubtedly uneasy about the rise of China as an economic, political and military rival. The two countries have a poisoned history. Japan was a surging force in the 1970s and 1980s, with esteemed commentators wondering whether it might overtake the US as an economy in the early twenty-first century and acquire the facets of a superpower. It would instead spend almost three decades in the doldrums and endure relative decline. That it maintained a trade surplus with the US, despite China moving into areas Japan had once led in, brought with it the risk of friction between Mr Trump and Tokyo. The Trans-Pacific Partnership that Japan had long championed found itself kicked into the long grass soon after Mr Trump took charge.

This did not lead to a damaging disagreement. For reasons that have never been fully divined, the then Japanese Prime Minister Shinzo Abe became one of Mr Trump's favourite overseas leaders, invited to his Florida resort and offered a round of golf with the President and friends. Whether that trick is bottled institutionally is improbable. The late Mr Abe's new successor in office, Shigeru Ishiba, already weakened by an insipid showing in a general election he called, would not appear to have the charisma or cunning needed to emulate Mr Abe's attributes.

Whether this creates angst depends on one of the real unknowns about the Trump II outlook. He drove South Korea and Japan to distraction with his courtship of Kim Jong Un and North Korea. Having begun by openly canvassing the prospect of 'fire and fury' if the 'rocket man' continued with intercontinental ballistic missile tests that might provide him with a means to hit US soil, Mr Trump spun around and met the Prince of Pyongyang three times (in Singapore in June 2018, Hanoi in February 2019 and the DMZ – taking a step into North Korea – in June 2019) before the improbable bromance ceased to be, with no deal on Kim abandoning nuclear weapons in sight. These engagements were staunchly opposed by much of the Republican foreign policy community and Japan was appalled at the spectacle. It suited President Moon Jae-in as he favoured a softly-softly approach to his counterpart in North Korea, but if it were to be repeated (as it might) then the South Korean political establishment would be extremely distressed.

So, from a lot further east, would be Australia and New Zealand. These are core US allies, but each had a bumpy ride in the first Trump Administration. The US President had a vocal row with Malcolm Turnbull, the Australian Prime Minister, over the terms of an agreement that Mr Obama had participated in which would mean the United States absorbing 1,250 refugees from camps in Nauru and Manus Island (Mr Trump did not wish to take them). They never made matters up but the next Australian Premier, Scott Morrison, steered any from trouble and was better liked.

The PM of New Zealand, Jacinda Ardern, a darling of the centre-left internationally, decided that discretion was the better part of valour (and upholding her exalted image) and met Mr Trump a small number of times, for the minimum period possible and with the least possible fanfare. She accepted an invitation to converse with Mr Biden and Ms Harris at the White House in 2022 with much more vigour.

It will fall, in a reversal of 2017–2021, for an Australian Prime Minister from the Labor Party, Anthony Albanese, and a New Zealand Prime Minister from the centre-right National Party, Christopher Luxon, to calculate what the interests of Oceania might be under Trump II.

If keeping China at bay is to be an American aim then, as the Biden Administration started to experiment with, there might be a means beyond South Korea and Japan that has strategic merit. Taking a thirty-to-fifty-year view of matters, then the VIPs (Vietnam, Indonesia and the Philippines) might be an interesting counterweight to Beijing in the economic and military contexts. They were not countries that seemed to fascinate anyone in the Trump camp from 2017 to 2021 (although the President himself was content to engage with Rodrigo Duterte in Manila, a leader whose attitude towards human rights and methodology in conducting his 'war on drugs' had made him a *persona non grata* in Mr Obama's foreign policy). But there was no bigger bite here.

It is possible that there might be if the more sophisticated end of the anti-China contingent has sway over the President in his second stint in office. While it is not easy to envision Tô Lâm, the General Secretary of the Communist Party of Vietnam, welcomed to the White House lawn, the new President of Indonesia, Prabowo Subianto (a General and self-styled right-wing nationalist), and the comparatively fresh Ferdinand 'Bongbong' Marcos Jr of the Philippines (a slick populist conservative) might be to Mr Trump's taste and presented as of an ilk with the Argentine leader.

Taiwan, which is not really sure what to expect of Mr

Trump and whether it can rely on him to be its protector (and if so at what cost in regards to its present supremacy in superconductors, which even the mild-mannered Biden Administration wanted to see translated into the building of incomprehensibly expensive facilities and factories in the United States itself). It frets whether it might end up as a handy bargaining chip if Mr Trump overrules most of those who will be around him, and treats China and its President in exclusively transactional terms, with Taiwan told firmly not even to muse about independence in private if it is to retain the military solidarity of the US.

The missing piece of the jigsaw in this critical corner is India. It might be a fellow member of what was originally (now much extended) the BRICS (Brazil, Russia, India, China and South Africa) but it has had tense border disputes with China in the past. Beijing has traditionally been aligned with Pakistan, ordinarily India's nemesis, and New Delhi has ambitions to become the sort of economic powerhouse that China is set upon cementing for itself (with the suspicion that there is not room for two such Asian dynamos in economic and political clout).

Some American Presidents (including, when India was a vastly more impoverished country, John F. Kennedy) have seen New Delhi as an enticing prospect that is worthy of the US assisting in its ascent. Others (including Ronald Reagan) did not seem to notice it at all. What is now the largest country in the world by population (having overtaken China) might well be logically thought of, as George H. W. Bush declared of Beijing well before its pursuit of power and prosperity, 'too big to ignore'. It has an underdeveloped military (notably a nominal navy) which, if senior American leaders were sufficiently dynamic, might have a seminal influence in the balance of military forces in the sea lanes of southern Asia.

A more visionary attitude in Washington could deliver it dividends. There are prizes that could be dangled, such as American support for India to become a member of the G7 or, which would be more complicated to realise, a permanent member of the United Nations Security Council. The first would put it one up on China economically. The second would render it as a political equal.

On this score, Mr Trump can be rated as ahead of the curve. Whether it be because of his past business dealings or personal connections, from the early days of his emergence as a political creature he has been enchanted by India. He spoke highly of its Prime Minister Narendra Modi of the nationalist Bharatiya Janata Party while on the campaign trail in 2015–2016, pledging to an audience of Indian Americans that if he won relations with India would be the 'best ever'.

These would not be mere words. Although there was some disharmony over trade (there are few countries with whom Mr Trump did not have some dispute over trade in his first term), this was an affectionate dialogue that had the smack of a love-in about it. India has an open door to the Administration. Where there were questions on which they might fall out, they were skirted.

The personal accord between the President and the Prime Minister was also obvious. If either man is inclined to engage in flattery, then, to borrow from Benjamin Disraeli in his liaison with Queen Victoria, they have no compunction in laying it on with a trowel. Mr Modi had a rather triumphal tour of the United States including a 'Howdy Modi' event in Houston, Texas which was cross-cultural in the extreme, but a big win for the Indian leader domestically as it was beamed to a (possibly bemused) electorate at home. Mr Trump went to India in February 2020. As COVID-19 was to strike shortly afterwards, it was the last major overseas visit of his first term.

India put on a show worthy of Bollywood. The diplomatic kitchen sink as well as the Taj Mahal was thrown at him. It had been labelled 'the Grand Visit'. It certainly was that.

A reprise of the Trump White House is an opening for India and an opportunity for the United States to forge a relationship with New Delhi that may become ever more significant over time. Mr Modi has been chastened by an election in 2024 which he had been expected to storm by a giant margin, yet which actually fell far short of that showing and so left him having to cobble together a parliamentary majority in a less than elevated fashion. Repackaging himself on the world stage would be a bonus for him. Mr Trump looks ready to provide him with that platform.

This renders one other potentially pivotal but extremely uncertain relationship in the wider world, which Mr Trump could not sideline even if he wanted to, but actually looks actively ready to examine: Russia.

As of today, it is difficult not to think of Russia – as if in a word association game – with Ukraine. If the restoration of Mr Trump to the Oval Office spurs what will be packaged as a peace settlement (perhaps an outcome that neither Moscow nor Kyiv has any affection for, but they can live with), what will be the engagement between the United States and Russia thereafter? Will personal contacts between Mr Trump and Vladimir Putin be reset? Will there be a version of side-letters, overt or covert, between Washington and Moscow so as to bring Mr Putin and the elites around him out of the crushing sanctions that they have been forced to adjust to, and back to old times?

This is an incendiary area. Mr Trump by inclination is probably closer to the Chinese leadership in favouring letting Mr Putin back in from the cold. Yet this would be opposed by the Chancellor of Germany, the President of France and

Prime Minister of the United Kingdom (never mind what other leaders whose territory is much more proximate to Russia will think).

Despite the appearance of an alliance, Mr Trump in his opening four years darted between being tough on Russia (additional sanctions in 2017 and stark opposition to the Nord Stream 2 gas pipeline which Germany, unwisely as matters were to develop, saw as its shortcut to cheap energy) and being softer with Moscow (reconsidering whether its seizure of Crimea was illegitimate, and floating the notion at the G7 Summit in Paris in 2019 that Russia be let back into that gathering). Which way Mr Trump jumps will depend in part on whether Ukraine impasse is resolved and, if not, whom he blames the most for a stalemate in dialogue and any more warfare on the ground. This is a decision with incredible implications beyond the security guarantees for Kyiv. Is Mr Putin a permanent pariah or will he be allowed a limited licence to return to the global stage?

This *Around the World in 4,000 Words* has been intended to illustrate that Mr Trump's influence will be extensive during the rest of this decade. Thanks to Elon Musk, there is now Outer Space too.

CHAPTER TWELVE

TRUMP AND THE UNITED KINGDOM

*Politics, economics and national security tie
Westminster to Washington*

The United Kingdom and the United States have a very long and continuing history. For most of the time since Britain conceded defeat in the War of Independence it has been a cordial one. There have been exceptions to this, such as the War of 1812 when what is now called the White House was set alight (it was more of a Brown House before the post-arson painting took place), the American Civil War (when much of the elite in the UK sympathised with the confederacy, despite slavery, because it stood for free trade unlike the North which favoured protectionism) and egos were bruised as the US overtook the UK as the largest economy in the world in the 1880s. Relations were thus a little distant and formal at the time of the American entry into World War I (although the extra resources this brought with it proved to be decisive in 1918). America withdrew from international engagement thereafter to focus on its own prosperity (New York replaced London as the most important financial centre on the planet in the 1920s). The ties of blood, however (more than half of US citizens then and still around a third today, traced their family roots back to the British Isles), ensured that the relationship remained a strong one.

It would not, though, in 1938 have been dubbed 'special' or any word similar in spirit to it. The contemporary interdependence of the UK and the US (frequently as this chapter will outline, the dependence of the UK on the US) was a product of World War II and the Cold War that followed. This is now more than eighty years old. Britain's place in a world order remains embedded in it.

To set out what the Trump Effect on the UK might be, requires as a first step, an audit of the UK as a political, economic, intellectual, cultural and military entity. Talking about oneself is not a very British activity to undertake. It is positively frowned upon in many circles. As a result, to an extent that is certainly not true of the United States, many in the UK have only a sketchy view of what the core characteristics of their own country are and what makes their nation distinctive. Those who occupy ministerial office, or who serve as diplomats, or at the helm of companies are not that much more enlightened about the UK either. A swift Audit of Britain is thus needed.

The United Kingdom is a country which punches well above its weight (as will be demonstrated) but has a glass jaw (it is less of an independent planet among countries than a big satellite of one). It covers 0.048% of the surface of the Earth, contains 0.851% of its population and 3.331% of its GDP (figures correct at the time of writing, but only the first is reliably pretty much constant over time). It has in London the largest urban economy in Europe (and only Moscow and Istanbul have a more sizeable population) which, according to the Global Financial Centres Index, is placed second in that regard to New York (that ranking has been retained for a century) with Paris back in tenth, Frankfurt ranked 18 and Milan a distant 45. More financial capital is under de facto control within 20 square miles of London than in the remaining cumulative 3.93 million square miles of Europe to the Urals.

In political terms, what is significant about the United Kingdom is that it is one of only five permanent members of the United Nations Security Council, has Embassies in 154 other countries (which puts it fourth behind China on 173, the US on 168 and France on 158), and is one of a mere five countries which are officially recognised and authorised nuclear weapons states (a club including the US, Russia, China and France, but with India, Pakistan, Israel and North Korea operating in its shadows). The UK is also a member of the G7 and the G20 and the IMF, World Bank and OECD, and a very long collection of other international organisations. It also has a card of its own in having created and remaining committed to the Commonwealth (which is underrated as an institution: it does, after all, involve India). The UK's Head of State (Charles III) also has that standing in fourteen other nations. Above all else, it is seen not only by itself but within the wider international community, as having a unique alliance with the United States, the actor which for now, and longer if it wishes, is the one true superpower in the world.

That is actually rather impressive. It meant that there was a moment around twenty years ago when – with Russia having cratered, China yet to start its economic Long March, and France being almost as aloof from the Americans under Jacques Chirac as it was when run by Charles de Gaulle – the UK could be designated as the second most important country in the world after the US, but about as far back as Glint of Gold behind Shergar in the 1981 Derby (the premier UK flat horse race). This could not be reasserted in the mid-2020s, but the UK is, nonetheless, a real global power.

This is aided and abetted by an economy which, while obviously not what it once was, still remains noteworthy. The UK has the sixth largest economy in the world behind those of the US, China, Japan, Germany and India, although it is almost the same in GDP as France. This makes it the second largest economy in Europe after Germany (and the biggest by far outside of the EU). It is the fourth largest exporter overall in the world and second largest exporter of services globally.

It is also, more than two hundred years after Napoleon initially made the dismissive comment, in a sense a 'nation of shopkeepers'. As of 2024 there were about 5.5 million businesses that were registered in the UK (the overwhelming majority of which are micro in employees) which is more than one in every ten residents of the nation (the highest such ratio in the G20). This is a rise from 3.5 million two decades earlier. The British have an entrepreneurial bug it would seem. The economy is utterly dominated by services (82%) and by financial services in particular. This can be both a strength and a weakness, as its exposure to the meltdown of 2008–2009 showed.

The relatively small manufacturing side of the economy is actually an item of some beauty. The UK has the second largest aerospace industry in the world. It has an intriguing automobile sector with stand-out brands such as Aston Martin, Bentley, Rolls-Royce, Jaguar Land Rover and Lotus. Its pivotal place in motor sport (Formula One is in effect based in the UK and more than 4,000 companies are connected to it) provides a £93 billion turnover and £22 billion value add. Eight out of ten cars made in the UK are sold overseas. The second and seventh most sizeable pharmaceutical companies on the planet are located in Britain. For a country where less than a tenth of the economy ranks as pure manufacturing, this is a robust record of 'making things'.

It is an exporter and importer on a grand scale. The largest single export market is the United States (in August 2024 the sum stood at a £4.13 billion), then Germany (£2.57 billion), the Netherlands (£2.16 billion), Ireland (£1.79 billion) and

Switzerland (£1.56 billion). Imports at the same date came in from Germany (£5.65 billion), China (£5.51 billion), the United States (£4.24 billion), the Netherlands (£3.92 billion) and France (£2.75 billion). The British have run a large trade deficit in goods with almost all developed economies for decades (not much public or political discussion of this occurs), and, critically in the light of Trump II, this (just about) includes the United States of America in most years. The UK is not on the 'naughty stool' with Team Trump in this terrain (inconveniently, 2024 may see a UK surplus).

That US export market is monumental. It is 17.6% of UK exports overall (27.2% in services). In 2023, around 40,100 UK VAT-registered businesses exported to the United States, a shade under a third of all those that exported anything, anywhere. More than a million jobs involve UK exports to America.

Precisely what the UK exports is also an aspect of national life which will come as a surprise.

The single largest export product is gold. Very little of it is mined in the UK. Despite this, the country is the second largest exporter of gold in proportionate terms (after Switzerland) and the fourth biggest in cash volume (after the Swiss again, the US, and, narrowly, the United Arab Emirates). Gold wins the export gold medal because London has been the world hub for the trade in physical bullion for an eternity and relies on the open, mostly unregulated, exchange of it for these exports to exist. After the yellow and shiny stuff (worth £25.7 billion in 2022), comes cars (£23.5 billion), gas turbines (£23.4 billion), crude petroleum (£21.0 billion) and products aligned to pharmaceuticals (£16.2 billion). If all forms of food and drink were stapled together statistically, they would be a big contender here. This list excludes financial services and professional services as an 'invisible'; otherwise the pair of these would rank among the highest by value, although calculating it with precision is often difficult.

If the measure is the spheres in which the UK is the largest single exporter anywhere in the world, then, by an intergalactic distance, the most prominent is the export of alcoholic spirits (£8 billion), and then the somewhat oddball set of horses (£535 million), collectors' items (£377 million), scrap nickel (£182 million) and scrap lead (£74.4 million). Booze, nags and bric-a-brac rule OK, UK. Whether there is any logical explanation for this idiosyncratic assortment of items is far beyond this analysis.

The fundamental point is that the UK is an exceptionally open economy (only the Netherlands and Finland are arguably even more free trade in orientation) and is vastly engaged with others. This is compounded by foreign direct investment (FDI) both out and in, with the United States as the most important player for the United Kingdom (even when the big EU economies are considered). In 2022, the outward stock of FDI from the UK to the US was £511.5 billion (or 26.9% of the total). In that year the inward stock of FDI from the US to the UK was £702.5 billion (a stunning 34% of the total tally).

The UK is also a serious force in technology, including the cutting-edge future elements of it. This sector is valued at $1 trillion (third behind the US, but by a big street, and of late China). If the comparison is with Europe, there is no contest. The tech sector in the UK is more than three times the size of France's, four times that of Germany and more than four times that of Italy. It has (although the last few years have been famine, not feast) a lot more venture capital behind it than any of its European counterparts, with much of that backing being American in origin.

The intellectual and cultural aspects to the United Kingdom

as a place and a polity matter too.

Britain's elite schools (although they involve children coming in) are a noteworthy export niche (VAT on school fees may make this yet more so). It is in higher education that the UK (other than the US) rules the roost. The findings of the respected QS World University Rankings 2024 were that four of the top ten universities globally are located in the UK (Oxford, Cambridge, Imperial College, London and University College, London), and also 17 of the foremost 100 universities (France has only four of them, so does Germany, Italy has none). If higher education could be calibrated as an export, such is the intensity of the magnet that is a university degree issued by an institution in this country that it would be placed as second after financial services. There is also an intangible value in hundreds of thousands of atypically intelligent young people coming to the United Kingdom and spending three or more years of their time and their money here (although convincing successive Home Secretaries of this has been something of a trial). An added benefit is that some of these people stay in the UK or if they return home (or head for North America) they are disproportionately inclined to conduct academic research with UK citizens.

The UK, or more correctly its men and women in white coats, has obtained the largest number of Nobel Prizes in the sciences and medicine after the US; it is also the second most significant centre globally for medical research and ranks third for published scientific research (after America and China). Not bad for a nation whose political elite consists of arts graduates.

This record adds to the UK's stock of what has come to be known as 'soft power'. Some of this is hard to put a numerical valuation on but it is real all the same. This involves being the home of the English language, having a convenient time zone between North America and East Asia and the English common law tradition which has had an immense influence (including in the US). Much of this relates to what the world watches, what it reads and what, if it chooses, it sings.

On these considerations, the UK is little less than a cultural superpower. It has an exceptional profile in film, literature (Shakespeare is serving the country well even though he died in 1616), sport (the British invented or set down the rules for most of them – American innovations such as baseball, the US version of football and basketball have not found as massive a set of markets), rock music (the Beatles bring in export income despite splitting up in 1970) and the theatre (the West End of London is a serious rival to New York in the audience figures that it draws in). The BBC is an enormous source of soft power, much more loved overseas than it can sometimes be at home. All this (plus tourism) collectively creates the sense of what a country is in the eyes of others. Soft power is, therefore, not soft in the sense of being weak. It is to be envied (and the UK is envied).

It does not render hard power inconsequential. The coming of Trump II, a President for whom hard power is very much the advantage that he will seek to maximise, will be critical. Democrats, as a rule, place weight on soft power. Republicans favour the heavier version.

So, it is the security element of the US–UK relationship that is absolutely vital to UK power.

It is the essence of what Winston Churchill (half-British, half-American through his mother and made an honorary US citizen in the last years of his life at the initiative of President Kennedy) coined the 'special relationship' in the 1940s, a phrase that has been repeated by almost every British Prime Minister ever since (the Europhile Edward Heath did not care for the terminology, resorting to a 'natural relationship' between the two nations as an alternative). It is what makes the State Department the first port of call for the UK Foreign Office (or more recently the UK Foreign, Commonwealth and Development Office) and the Pentagon the mother ship for the UK Ministry of Defence. Without the close ties that were established in World War II and then the Cold War (when George Orwell thought of three superpowers after 1945: the United States, the USSR and the British Empire and Commonwealth), the UK might well punch above its weight, but it would not have the same clout. It makes who is living in the White House a matter of not merely national interest but national imperative. In the military domain, this is coinage of high value.

The foundations of the intelligence community alliance, both the bilateral one between the US and the UK and the 'five eyes' including Australia, Canada and New Zealand in some spheres, rest on the BRUSA Agreement of 1943 (virtually unknown on either side of the Atlantic) and the UKUSA Agreement of 1946, followed later by the US–UK Mutual Defence Agreement of 1958 which covers nuclear weapons co-operation, and a long practice of privileged access to military procurement (at its simplest the US sells to the UK what it would not be willing to sell to others). This has been supplemented by other treaties and accords between leaders too numerous to list.

One aspect of this is military bases. There remain American personnel at RAF Menwith Hill, Fylingdales, Lakenheath, Mildenhall (due to close in 2027), Fairford (the only base for American strategic bombers in Europe), Croughton and Welford. The Brits do not want 'Yankee Go Home'. That these establishments are still assets some 35 years after the Cold War ended is telling. The UK and the US share bases at Diego Garcia in the Indian Ocean and Ascension Island in the Atlantic Ocean. Although rarely making the news headlines, they are seminal to naval supremacy.

This has not been a relationship of equals at any point in the last eight decades and it clearly is not now. It is absolutely essential to the UK but more of a worthy convenience to the Americans. It has caused Prime Ministers to engage in contortions or episodes of self-imposed silence. Harold Wilson ducked and weaved to avoid committing any British troops to Vietnam (the Australians were not so fortunate), Margaret Thatcher might have interacted enthusiastically with Ronald Reagan but had her troubles with him over the Falkland Islands, the US invasion of Grenada (a Commonwealth country) and the extent of his later zeal for eliminating the risk of nuclear war in concert with Mikhail Gorbachev. Tony Blair threw in his lot with George W. Bush on Iraq as being inside the tent stuck him as the best option but saw his status at home scarred savagely for his decision.

The asymmetry today is spectacular. This is because while the United States has maintained and at times has increased its gigantic spending on defence (more than virtually everyone else who counts put together), the UK has tried to reduce it, especially in relation to troop numbers.

The British are not shirkers and slackers in military expenditure by any means. We stand sixth in such spending in cash (after the US, China, Russia, India and a smidge behind Saudi Arabia) but the recent trend has been to substitute people in uniform for high technology within defence.

As of 2023, there were a little more than 140,000 active UK military personnel (supported by around 45,000 others in the overall Armed Forces). The Army had 80,000 men and women (a low number historically, about the capacity at Old Trafford), the Royal Navy just over 32,000, the RAF about 31,000.

For context, since the year 2000 this constitutes a cut of 28% for the Army, 26% for the Royal Navy and Marines and a whopping 45% for the Royal Air Force. The pace of reduction has not slowed. The overall figures fell by around 3% from 2023 to 2024. All three services are actually below the personnel levels assigned to them and are attempting to secure additional recruits. Churn has become a major challenge. The Armed Forces and family life are not an easy blend. The dash to rely on expensive hardware and high technology has had some almost comical by-products. For instance, it was decided that it was vital for the Royal Navy to have two new aircraft carriers to replace ones that were ancient and increasingly ineffective. They were built and are at sea (HMS *Queen Elizabeth* and HMS *Prince of Wales*) but came in late and so way over budget (the combined cost was £7.6 billion) that the Ministry of Defence has often struggled to be able to fund the aircraft to put on them and raided other service budgets to do it.

In the military realm as of 2024, the old cliché of the United States and the United Kingdom acting as an international Batman and Robin is hard to reconcile with the size of UK forces. It is more like Batman and Alfred Pennyworth, his fictional butler (a former British special forces officer in the story). Although not as ostentatiously as other European nations, the UK has been penny-pinching on defence for ages.

It will not be able to carry on in this manner for much longer. What this overview will hopefully have indicated is that the Trump Effect is about far more than the extent to which the once and present President will say or do things that the average Labour Party activist finds appalling, with the Labour government desperately seeking to avoid disagreement with the White House, to the annoyance of constituency parties (although it is an absolute certainty this will be witnessed). The arrival of Trump II, different in form from Trump I, is a much bigger shift of tectonic plates.

The issues where this will be of consequence are many, varied and of exceptional significance.

At its most basic, the United Kingdom as a country whose authority is amplified by transnational institutions and multi-lateralism (and more complicated in this light after the Brexit referendum) has a vested stake in transnationalism and multi-lateralism. The Trump Administration did not see matters the same way between 2017 and 2021 and will be firmer still in that view from 2025. The UK will doubtless aspire to recast its traditional notion of itself as a 'bridge' between the United States and the European continent, but might find itself a bridge without a waterway below.

As an economy, the United Kingdom, extremely open and a champion of free trade for almost two hundred years now, also has a massive stake in the status quo. It is no longer allied to the largest trade bloc in the world (the European Union single market and customs union) and has yet to come close to an autonomous free trade deal with the US that might be an alternative. It (like Europe overall, to be fair) sits uneasily between the United States and China, involved with them both economically and with no wish to be obliged to choose one over the other (but no credible option if push came to a sufficiently hard shove but to stick with the US). As sterling is barely a reserve currency any longer, it is hostage to the movements of the dollar.

A trade war with tariffs of 20% introduced across the board by Trump II with a resulting shrinking in the overall volume of international trade would be a nightmare for this or any UK government. The one argument it could make is that as, highly unusually, the UK does not run a trade surplus in goods with the United States, it may negotiate some sort of exemption for itself in key sectors (a not impossible outcome). If it pulled this trick off, however, it would have minimal effect on the world economy and international trading order and would be the proverbial lead balloon for the UK in its relationship with European trading partners. Trumponomics is an area of deep angst.

In the military space, the UK is also exposed by an emboldened Republican rule in Washington. The immediate crisis involves Ukraine. If the Americans turn off the taps to Kyiv what could London, Berlin, Paris, Warsaw and others do in response? Do they shrug their shoulders and tell Ukraine that, sadly, it will have to surrender territory in order to reach a settlement with Russia? If not, how much more money will the UK (and others) really be willing to come up with in order to keep Ukraine viable on the battlefield and what kinds of changes in the rules of engagement would Whitehall envisage to assist Kyiv further but at the risk of a direct conflict with Moscow? What is the UK to do about its many frozen Russian assets if the Americans release those that they hold?

This is but a dress rehearsal for the real dilemma which comes with defence expenditure. In anticipation of either a Trump triumph or any Democratic President also becoming far more irritated with allies, the UK had, with Sir Keir Starmer making the case personally, agreed to embrace a 2.5% target for defence spending but with a sketchy timetable. This may well not be a large enough figure, and it may have to be seen to be delivered swiftly. What does that do for the Budget that Rachel Reeves, serving as Chancellor, produced in October 2024 and for the Treasury later? A multi-year cross-departmental spending review due in Spring 2025 may need some revisions.

Trump II is an event of transformational significance for the United Kingdom. Yet, it cannot be avoided. Much of what it involves can be anticipated (as it has in this volume). Other facets of it are unknown as of today. The UK does know that it will be close to the eye of the coming storm.

CONCLUSION

TRUMP, TRUMPISM AND TRUMPISM
AFTER TRUMP

*The five factors that will shape the next four
years for America and the world*

There is no relevant precedent for what Washington, D.C. is about to experience. The single example of a former President returning to office after being defeated for re-election is that of Grover Cleveland, who had won the office in 1884. He lost in 1888 in a controversial fashion to his rival Benjamin Harrison over the issue of tariffs (the Democrat Cleveland wanted to make swingeing cuts in them, the Republican Harrison did not) even though the sitting President had carried the popular vote (the last time the electoral college would malfunction in this respect until 2000) amid dark suggestions of corruption and electoral mischief being made by Mr Cleveland's fans. He had a comeback victory in 1892 over Mr Harrison but did not stand again in 1896 as he was entirely within his rights to do (the XXIInd Amendment imposing a two-term limit came in 1951).

This is so long ago, the federal government so much smaller and America's place in the world so utterly different to that of today that it is of absolutely no use in evaluating modern politics.

The following five fundamental factors are what we should instead be working with for analysis.

The first, as has hopefully been hammered home in these

pages, is that what will occur is much better thought of as a second first term than anything akin to a conventional second term. As set out earlier, this time round Mr Trump starts life as a Category A President, not a Category B one, as the Senate moved in his direction while the Republicans just kept hold of the House of Representatives. He also prevailed in the popular vote in 2024, unlike 2016, so there is no sense in which his legitimacy can now be disputed. The claim to a mandate is much stronger. He has stronger foundations this time. A CBS News poll released almost three weeks after his victory showed that a full 31% of Americans were 'happy' about his restoration and 24% were 'satisfied' (better than in 2016). More Republicans were 'excited' at his coming tenure than eight years earlier (more Democrats were scared). A solid 59% approved of how he had handled the transition so far (despite some contentious nominations, one of whom had to withdraw very quickly). Of his signature policies, tariffs won narrow 52%–48% support, mass deportation of illegal immigrants a clearer 57%–43% backing.

The second is that this is a narrow window of opportunity. If history is any steer, then it will last for two years, not the full four-year term. The Democrats will be heavily favoured to win back the House of Representatives in the mid-term elections of 2026 (it would be an awesome result for the Republicans to retain that chamber), which means Mr Trump would again be back in Category C. The Senate will be competitive in that there will be 33 regular elections there and at least two extra special elections (to fill the shoes of Vice President Vance in Ohio and Secretary of State Rubio in Florida), which means the Republicans are defending 22 seats and Democrats only 13 seats. The two most vulnerable-looking races, however, are in Georgia and Michigan, which the Democrats hold at the moment. Maine would also be in this camp if the Republican

Susan Collins were to retire. The odds, therefore, are that the Republicans are best placed to keep the US Senate after 2026.

Irrespective of who wins where, after two years Mr Trump will not be the figure that he is in 2025. The sands of political time will be slipping away from him. The race to replace him will have started. On the Republican side all eyes will be on the Vice President whose prominence is a huge asset. Mr Rubio might chance his arm as well (but Secretary of State is a terrible base for a presidential nomination bid in the Republican Party). Senator Rick Scott of Florida may fancy himself (and he is rich enough to subsidise himself). Governor Glenn Youngkin of Virginia also has a large private piggy bank, which is helpful. Governor Kim Reynolds of Iowa is a darling of many devoted conservative activists. Do not discount Donald Trump Jr musing whether he can make a run for it. On the Democrat side the field is completely open, with ex-Vice President Harris probably rendered a busted flush.

Those around Mr Trump can make the above calculations too. They need to move hard and fast. In domestic politics in particular the first eighteen months of this term will prove to be decisive.

The third element is that the Trump White House and Administration should be better organised and more ideological than last time. The new Chief of Staff, Susie Wiles, an ex-lobbyist, is a real operator. She introduced some sort of firm order into Mr Trump as a candidate for the third time (imposing discipline on what he said at campaign rallies would be a miracle worthy of Jesus) and unlike others who have served him in that function, Mr Trump plainly trusts her. He has (after a bouncy ride in certain cases) acquired Cabinet nominees and other key figures who are of his choosing this time rather than being snookered by the GOP establishment in 2017. The litmus test now is personal loyalty to the

President himself more than any other feature. There will be a unity and determination about Trump II that was scarcely there for Trump I.

Those nominees offer a fascinating insight into the fault lines of the new Trump Administration. In foreign policy, the two most important are Marco Rubio as Secretary of State (if as one would expect he is confirmed) and Mike Waltz, the incoming National Security Adviser (an internal White House position so no senatorial scrutiny and vote required). Mr Rubio, a Florida Senator from 2011, and Cuban-American by birth, has a dense record of statements and action on international matters (although he has trimmed his sails to stay close to Mr Trump of late). He was very influential on US policy towards Latin America between 2017–2021 (in part because neither Mr Trump nor Mr Pompeo as Secretary of State had strong views on the subject) and was seen as a hawk on the Middle East, favouring a vigorous US role in Afghanistan, Libya, Iraq, Syria and Yemen (but has toned that down). He was similarly an early and loud champion of Ukraine (but now refers to the situation there as a 'stalemate' best ended). He is certainly and consistently a foe of China, and across a wide range of controversies. He is mirrored by Mr Waltz (who until his recent elevation was a Florida congressman), who initially endorsed a US long-haul in Afghanistan (where he had served as a Colonel in the US Army) but now sees that as a lost cause. His higher priority is China, where he was among the most hostile figures in the House of Representatives.

The double-act in economics and trade is also an intriguing one. Mr Trump settled on Scott Bessent to put forward as Treasury Secretary. He was a relatively conventional Wall Street sort of choice (he has been an immensely successful hedge fund manager, cutting his teeth assisting George Soros in sinking the pound on Black Wednesday in 1992). He is a passionate advocate of the Trump tax cut agenda but rather more cautious in his utterances on tariffs, suggesting that the 20% figure that is often cited is 'maximalist' and that they are 'a useful negotiating tool'. His caution may matter little as Howard Lutnick, the incoming 'super Commerce Secretary' (in that he seems to have oversight of the Office of the US Trade Representative, which is to be led by Jamieson Greer, an ex-Chief of Staff there in the first Trump Administration, as well), and head of the leading financial institution Cantor Fitzgerald (a company that recovered from losing 658, or 70%, of its brokers in the Twin Towers attack of September 11 2001, including Mr Lutnick's own brother) is deeply committed to tariffs as much more than a negotiating tool. The division of spoils here is clear. Mr Bessent will be Mr Tax Cuts. Mr Lutnick will be Mr Tariff Increases.

Fourth, although he has a bold (and contentious) agenda at home, it is also a limited one. His priorities will be nailing down the cuts in tax that are contained in the Tax Cuts and Jobs Act of 2017 (and which will expire at the end of 2025 if they do not have a fresh legal renewal) and then extending them further through the host of campaign pledges explored in Chapter Six. A very close second in terms of urgency will be border security and completing the wall across the whole of the boundary with Mexico, which Mr Trump yearns for. He has a solid shot at getting his way. Recasting the federal bureaucracy to ensure its loyalty and shutting down the 'deep state' might be beyond him, but he will acquire more opportunities to reshape the Supreme Court with as many as three nominations (and perhaps even a replacement for Chief Justice John Roberts) as plausible possibilities. If so, he will be the most significant President on the courts since FDR. This is a substantial roster but not the scale of FDR overall, Lyndon Johnson or Ronald Reagan. Mr Trump at home will be of considerable importance but he will not remake the United States.

It is the world beyond America where the Trump Effect could be enormous. As set out in this tome, he may transform the terms of international trade through the assertive use of tariffs, could marginalise multilateralism, abandon Ukraine, compel NATO allies to raise expenditure on defence by a lot more than they are assuming, challenge China on multiple fronts, shake up the Middle East once more (or be shaken up himself by it) including escalating the American confrontation with Iran and also make the weather in the Americas, South and East Asia, with Russia and its neighbours, and in many more places besides this.

Nor is this simply about 'wake me up when these four years are over.' Mr Trump and Trumpism have become the credo of the Republican Party. That will not end when he eventually has to pack in the presidency and head back to Florida to enjoy his golf into his dotage. He will shift the Democratic Party in his direction too as it searches its soul for why he has been so effective with white working-class Americans (and in 2024 with a sudden surge of support among Latino men as well). The aftershocks of the Trump era on how the United States sees itself and its role in the world will be greater than the ages of Clinton, both Bushes, Obama and Biden combined.

Trump II, in summary, has the capacity to be transformative. What this will mean is to be seen.

POSTSCRIPT

A STRATEGY FOR BRITAIN, 2025–2029

The re-election of Donald Trump demands fresh thinking from those at the helm in Whitehall because, although his second term will last just four years (a not inconsiderable stretch and one that may well match the entire life of the UK government elected in July 2024), what can be described as Trumpism will continue to influence the Republican Party very directly, the Democratic Party more indirectly and hence American politics and policy well beyond 2029.

What, in practical terms, should the UK Prime Minister, government and political class now do?

The first chance that Sir Keir Starmer has been afforded to set out his approach at any length was through his address at the Lord Mayor's Banquet at the Guildhall on 2 December 2024. This occasion has long been associated with international affairs, not domestic politics. It has also allowed the Prime Minister the chance to be more philosophical and less overtly partisan.

In that regard, Sir Keir did not disappoint. He made his argument in admirably clear terms. It is worth setting out what direction he would like to take and then modestly offer him navigation.

In his opening remarks, the Prime Minister referred to the recent 'record-breaking' international investment conference that he had hosted as evidence of 'why our global relationships matter so much to this country'. He also noted that the conduct of foreign policy was very challenging. He mused that 'geopolitics is on our doorstep' (it is actually through the door and is the carpet of the property). He conceded that there was public disquiet as a consequence and a desire to 'take back control of our lives, our borders, our livelihoods'. Although he did not make the link explicitly, he could have asserted that the sentiment above largely explained Mr Trump's victory.

He also admitted that the world had changed dramatically and not for the better. In an echo of the thesis set out in this volume in Chapter Two, he contended that 'There was a sense in the years of The Great Moderation that while the world always had conflicts, democratic values were in the ascendency.' Such confidence, he did not quite state candidly, no longer held.

In the aftermath of the Trump triumph, the Prime Minister was keen to stress continuity:

'The idea that we must choose our allies. That somehow we're with either America or Europe is plain wrong. I reject it utterly. Attlee did not choose between allies. Churchill did not choose. The national interest demands that we work with them both.'

Arguably both men did make an implicit choice in that they shunned the European Coal and Steel Community, which would evolve into the EEC, but in fairness they did not see it that way.

While some in his own camp might not be at ease with this approach with Mr Trump back in office, Sir Keir did not shirk from the situation. He continued his oration by stating:

'And that's why when President Trump graciously hosted me for dinner in Trump Tower, I told him that we would invest more deeply than ever in the transatlantic bond with our American friends in the years to come.'

Later in his text he would also refer to 'Even closer ties to the US' as he also sought to restore in part the link with the

European Union and its large member states such as France and Germany.

On the specific issues where friction with Washington could be expected, the Prime Minister made it plain that he wanted himself and the country to be a real player, not a mere participant.

Russia is, he intoned, a 'near and present danger'. This meant continued support for Kyiv. So:

'To put Ukraine in the strongest possible position for negotiations, so that they can secure a just and lasting peace on their terms and guarantee their security, independence – and right to choose their future.'

This form of words tacitly acknowledged that the United States under a restored President Trump will not be inclined to assist Ukraine in fighting to the finish but looking for a finish to it.

On NATO, which the Prime Minister praised to the hilt (unlike his predecessor as Labour leader), change and cash would need to be forthcoming if the credibility of the body were to remain.

He pointed out that 'almost £3 billion of additional resources for defence' had been set aside in the recent Budget (not a huge sum in truth) and that 'We will set out a clear path to increase spending from 2.3% of GDP today to 2.5%.' There was, however, no timetable for this increase but the assumption would continue to be that it would be contained within the next multi-year spending review which was unlikely to be revealed by the Chancellor much before June 2025.

The final potential sticky wicket was China. The Prime Minister acknowledged the tough pitch.

'It is remarkable that until I met President Xi last month there had been no face-to-face meeting between British and Chinese leaders for six years.'

This was unfortunate because:

'We can't simply look the other way. We need to engage. To co-operate, to compete and to challenge on growth, on security, on climate as well as address our differences in a full and frank way on issues like Hong Kong, human rights and sanctions on our parliamentarians.'

There was no definitive statement, though, that the UK did not have to and would not have to choose between America and China. This is not an implausible prospect (although hardly a welcome thought in Whitehall) and it would not be much of a choice in the end. It is the US.

With that, Sir Keir sought to draw his ambitions together in a peroration for his audience:

'When it comes to our role in the world today, I want to recapture that sense of pride. To stand tall once again. To meet people's concerns not with easy answers, which don't serve anyone, but with leadership. To face up to the world as it is, shape it in our interests, and deliver more growth, more security and stronger alliances.'

Adopting what Philip Larkin had said of the late Queen Elizabeth II, the PM wanted the UK to be: '... a constant and responsible actor in turbulent times'.

Noble words. How might he, the government, and the nation as a whole turn them into action?

An activist agenda here is not an incredible notion but it will require both leadership and risk.

The most pressing item will probably be Ukraine. It is not difficult to envisage what the shape of a settlement might look like even if, as a matter of principle, it is not an attractive one. Mr Putin will not settle for anything less than tangible territorial concessions, the four provinces that are largely under the control of his forces as well as the international recognition of Crimea as the sovereign territory of the Russian state. He is also unlikely to favour the remaining majority of Ukraine being awarded NATO membership (although integration into the EU may be tolerable). Furthermore, under an American President who considers NATO to be 'obsolete', membership of it, were the Kremlin to concede it, would not be considered the enticing prize that it once was.

There have to be security guarantees of some sort, nonetheless, for any settlement to stick. The presence on the ground of troops which are drawn from NATO countries, even if not wearing the NATO badge or operating under its Charter (and the all-important Article Five doctrine that an attack on one NATO nation is, in effect, bar colonial and semi-colonial disputes, an attack on all 32 NATO members), would be a military presence which would offer some reassurances to Kyiv that any future Russian military assault would carry a real risk of internationalising the conflict.

In that light, the UK would be wise to be at the head of a 'coalition of the willing' among the European NATO members (and, if willing, Canada) establishing a force which would be seen as a buffer zone between Ukraine and a future Russian incursion. The numbers involved would be more than symbolic, but do not need to be substantial to achieve this objective. If the US were ready to offer air cover if required, then that would be all the more impressive as an exercise. It is not inconceivable that Mr Trump would allow this to occur (if he were not sent the invoice). The UK, combined with France, Germany, Poland and others, could make a difference here.

The second area where the UK should want to innovate is on defence spending. There is an argument that as it is not a shirker, it should not put its hand up first on this matter. This would be a mistake. The demand for better burden-sharing is not solely an obsession of Mr Trump or the Republican Party. It should be assumed that it will be held by a Democratic

Administration as well. The Prime Minister should separate the (inevitable) forthcoming rise in expenditure on national security from the broader detail of the multi-year spending review and announcement. The UK should commit early to 2.5% of GDP by a short-term date (2027 at the latest), set out a path to reach 3% not long after that (2029/2030) and make this a cash floor, not a ceiling. This will set a baseline for others. If NATO is to survive as a serious force, it has to make this move.

The third aspect of a proactive push by the United Kingdom involves its own trading stance with the United States. As the single largest trading partner and by far the most important bilateral partner on foreign direct investment, the UK has to maximise its economic engagement here and not hold back because others who run large surpluses in goods with the United States might be aggrieved if London manages to land itself with attractive terms. There may never be a better opening for a UK–US Free Trade Agreement than in the eighteen months or so after Mr Trump is back in the White House and the Republican Party holds both the Senate and the House of Representatives, but before mid-term elections in 2026 which will probably change these arrangements and usher in a lengthy campaign to be Mr Trump's successor in 2029. The UK needs to take this extremely seriously and appoint a heavyweight figure with stand-out business qualifications to be its chief negotiator as a Minister located in the House of Lords.

Fourth, there is an opening for the UK to serve as a 'bridge' but not between Europe and North America. That aspiration did not really deliver even when the UK was a major country within the European Union. It cannot be revisited unless a political party can stand for and win election on the explicit mission of rejoining the EU and then making the commitments needed for this to be seen on the continent as a much more wholehearted position than it was previously (which by implication would involve adopting the euro shortly after coming back to Brussels). Absent this scenario (which looks extremely unlikely but then again in 2010 the UK's departure from the EU would not have been anticipated either), then the 'bridge' concept verges on the rather fanciful. A bridge does, after all, need to be attached to a body of land and the UK is not fixed to the EU. This is not an argument against negotiating a better deal with the EU or moving closer to it but it is a forthright determination that this is nothing like the notion of a 'bridge', more a gangplank.

There is another bridge role that might be worth exploring. The UK could quite properly attempt to be the link between the United States and China. This notion could have potential if it turns out that Mr Trump is, as might well be the case, much more transactional in his approach towards China than the more ideological disposition of some of those around him and many not only in the Republican Party but sections of the Democrats too. If Mr Trump's overwhelming aim is to reduce the enormous trade surplus that China holds over the United States, then there is a degree of scope for someone to test out what he might be willing to offer (and China ready to accept) if there were to be some form of 'grand bargain' between the US and China on trade.

What sort of solution might be seductive? The UK could suggest that China's critical role in the world economy were recognised by bringing it into the G7 and other critical economic units such as the IMF, the World Bank and the OECD as a full and significant player. Mr Trump, who does not set much store by multilateralism, might view this as a modest bargaining chip to play. In a similar spirit, the UK might also loudly champion India as part of what would be a G9 (plus the EU and, conceivably, Russia, although that would not be enjoyable to swallow). It would mean that the G7 (or whatever number emerges) would represent the global economy rather better. There is the opportunity for a slick UK government to make itself central to a rapprochement between Washington and Beijing that would make for a more stable international community.

If the UK could obtain a taste for institutional innovation, then there are more kites here to fly.

The United Nations was founded in 1945 as an Anglo-American initiative. It originally had a Security Council consisting of five permanent members (the US, UK, France, the USSR (later Russia), China – originally the authorities in Taiwan, but then the People's Republic of China) and six of the remaining 46 other countries, who would rotate on a regional basis thereafter. In 1965, in part because the passing of two decades made it appear a sound moment to revisit its architecture, but also because overall membership had expanded from 51 to 117 countries, a reform was adopted which retained the P5 but expanded the Security Council to 15 overall. There has been no further reconsideration of the design for almost sixty years now despite the membership of the UN steadily increasing from 51 in 1945 to 117 by 1965 to 193 states today.

The UK could assert that the time for another review of the UN Security Council was overdue. There are at least two ways of doing this. The first would be to retain the existing P5 with the veto power but add another tier of nations which had permanent seats but no single veto (such as India, Japan, a Latin American country and an African state) and then the rotating members in a Security Council which was, for the sake of a number, 21 strong, or have an expansion of the P5 to a P7 (India and Japan would be the strongest contenders in economic and military assets), all with veto authority, as part of an expanded Security Council of between 19 and 21 members.

The logic for contemplating such a shift is compelling. It might take some time to occur (the 1965 amendment had a lengthy gestation period) but the UK would put credit in the bank by being prepared to be an international thought leader and willing to accept a small dilution of its own autonomy as a P5 member by allowing others a similar status (with or without a veto). If the UK wants to continue to 'punch above its weight', then it needs fast footwork inside of the ring. The British are good at inventing activities and then writing down the rules (with the notable exception of framing a national constitution, but never mind). We should revisit that talent.

Finally, an imaginative foreign policy for the next four years and for long after that should place even more emphasis than we currently do on 'soft power' in entrenching our influence. This is more important than most in the vital special relationship between the UK and the US in itself. At the Guildhall, the Prime Minister waxed lyrical about investing 'more deeply than ever in this transatlantic bond' with the United States and the virtue of 'even closer ties' with the US. What could he do in the immediate years ahead to turn sentences and sentiments into substance?

An answer, perhaps the answer, is to be found in a perhaps improbable and unpredicted place.

It is the Republican Party Platform for the 2024 presidential election. It comes in one single sentence. It sits within the overall text (America First: A Return to Common Sense), residing in Chapter Eight (Bring Common Sense to Government and Renew the Pillars of American Civilization), resting in section nine (Honor American History). It lies in this pledge:

'We will organize a National Celebration to mark the 250th Anniversary of the Founding of the United States of America.'

In other words, the year 2026 and, especially, the date of 4 July 2026 is scheduled to become a party. This is a huge opportunity for the United Kingdom (a nation whose idiosyncratic sense of humour and capacity for poking fun at itself is legendary and is also a source of soft power). We should celebrate the creation of the United States with it and in part independently as well.

There is a range of options here, but the main vehicle is renewing our links by diplomacy and twinning. The King and Queen should head to the United States in 2026 as should the soft power exports of the Prince and Princess of Wales and their young family. As the football/soccer World Cup will take place in the US (and Canada and Mexico) in the summer of 2026, Prince William, as the President of the Football Association will, hopefully, have more than one reason to be on American soil then. (We will park what to do about the Duke and Duchess of Sussex while their relatives are there for the time being.) The apparent chemistry between Mr Trump and the Prince of Wales when they met in Paris in December 2024 was striking. The visual impact, truly significant. Prince William may prove a better personal ambassador to the White House than any member of the UK Cabinet. He is more senior in age than J. D. Vance, which is a little surprising in that an American Vice President might be expected to be rather older than his very early forties.

This would be to repeat but to extend the trick of 1976 when, to mark the bicentennial of the United States, Queen Elizabeth II and the Duke of Edinburgh toured Philadelphia, Washington, New York City, New Haven, Charlottesville, Providence and Boston in a highly acclaimed trip. The 2026 visit should look beyond locations in the original thirteen colonies and focus on expanding and emerging US population centres. Mr Trump should be invited on a visit here in the same year in a reciprocation arrangement.

Institutional relationships should be deepened across the board. Academic institutions could twin with each other as cities and towns have long done. The same could be seen between companies and sectors in the corporate sphere. Sporting and cultural entities could also form a unique arrangement with one another. Families with the same surname across the pond could be encouraged to establish online networks. Following the 80th anniversary of the end of WWII in 2025, the trigger event in the emergence of the special relationship, a mutual marking of the American Revolution would surely be the convenient catalyst for it to be renewed.

And what would be more appropriate for the UK and US in the Age of Trump than showmanship? How Winston Churchill, the founding father of the special relationship, would heartily approve.

ABOUT THE AUTHOR

TIM HAMES was a Prize Research Fellow in American Studies at Nuffield College Oxford and a Lecturer in Politics at Christ Church and Oriel College in the 1990s. He was then an Assistant Editor, the Chief Leader Writer and a weekly columnist at *The Times*. Subsequent to that he was the Director General of the British Private Equity and Venture Capital Association (BVCA).

He co-authored (with Dame Kate Bingham) *The Long Shot* (the inside account of the success of the UK Vaccine Taskforce during the COVID-19 crisis). He is now a co-founder and a partner at Acuti Associates, a political/geopolitical advisory consultancy. He is a self-styled Trumpologist, meaning neither a Trumpapologist, nor a Trumpophobe, but a close student of the phenomena.

His next book *Measuring Monarchy: The most overrated and underrated British Kings and Queens* is scheduled for publication in summer 2025.

Printed in Great Britain
by Amazon

61638796R00119